THIS BOOK
BELONGS TO

....

....

©COPYRIGHT 2024

The content contained within this book may not be reproduced, duplicated, or transmitted without direct written permission from the author or the publisher. Under no circumstances will any blame or legal responsibility be held against the publisher, or author, for any damages, reparation, or monetary loss due to the information contained within this book. Either directly or indirectly.

Legal Notice:
This book is copyright protected. This book is only for personal use. You cannot amend, distribute, sell, use, quote, or paraphrase any part, or the content within this book, without the consent of the author or publisher.

Disclaimer Notice:
Please note the information contained within this document is for educational and entertainment purposes only. All effort has been executed to present accurate, up-to-date, and reliable, complete information. No warranties of any kind are declared or implied. Readers acknowledge that the author is not engaging in the rendering of legal, financial, medical, or professional advice. The content within this book has been derived from various sources. Please consult a licensed professional before attempting any techniques outlined in this book. By reading this document, the reader agrees that under no circumstances is the author responsible for any losses, direct or indirect, which are incurred as a result of the use of the information contained within this document, including, but not limited to — errors, omissions, or inaccuracies.

Did you like my book? I pondered it severely before releasing this book. Although the response has been overwhelming, it is always pleasing to see, read or hear a new comment. Thank you for reading this and I would love to hear your honest opinion about it. Furthermore, many people are searching for a unique book, and your feedback will help me gather the right books for my reading audience.

Thanks!

Table of Contents

Slow Cooker	5
Meat Dishes	9
Poultry Dishes	32
Seafood Dishes	54
Vegetarian / Vegan Dishes	76
Appetizers	100
Side Dishes	110
Desserts	116
Soups, Broths & Stocks	121

Slow Cooker

What is a Slow Cooker?

A slow cooker is a countertop electrical appliance that simmers food at a lower temperature than cooking methods such as frying, boiling and baking. This enables cooking to be left unattended for many hours without worrying about the food overcooking or burning. Nowadays there are many slow cooker brands, the most popular one is known as Crock-Pot.

The Benefits of Using a Slow Cooker

Easy and Quick: Slow cookers make cooking a healthy meal simple. All you have to do is put the ingredients into the slow cooker, set the timer and the temperature setting, and then wait for your meal to cook.

Saves money: A slow cooker doesn't use as much electricity as a regular electric stove, which not only saves money but is also good for the environment.

Healthy: Slow cookers often don't require you to use any fats or oils during the cooking process, so they cook healthier meals. A lot of the vitamins, nutrients and minerals are preserved because foods cook in their own juices.

Flavorful: Without you putting in a lot of effort, slow cookers produce more flavor than regular cooking. The food is left to cook for hours, and so the full flavor of sauces become richer as the flavor is released. The food is not cooked with a regular lid, but it is sealed onto the cooker and so there is no or little loss of flavor through evaporation.

Saves time: The only requirement of using a slow cooker is that you add all the ingredients in together; therefore it saves you time. You only need to use one kitchen utensil, so it also saves time cleaning up.

No burnt food: The food is cooked at a low temperature, so there is no chance of it getting burnt or sticking to the bottom of the pan.

Keeps the kitchen cool: A regular oven and stove not only cooks your food, it also cooks your kitchen! You don't have this problem with a slow cooker.

How to Use a Slow Cooker Properly

1) Make sure the temperature is set correctly. If you need to cook something quickly, set the temperature on high.
2) Place the slow cooker on a sturdy surface; it also helps if you set it on top of a tea towel to soak up any liquid that might spit or spill out of it.
3) Don't rest your slow cooker against a wall or too close to any other appliances because of the amount of heat that it produces.
4) Remove any leftovers from the cooker and transfer them into a container. Allow them to cool down before placing them in the refrigerator. Don't let food cool down in the slow cooker because it retains heat for a long time; while it's cooling, bacteria can build up.
5) Don't lift the lid up to check on your food. The heat lost will extend the cooking time for approximately 10 to 30 minutes.

Useful Tips for Using a Slow Cooker

- When using ingredients such as pasta, rice and fresh herbs, add them towards the end during the final 30 to 60 minutes.
- If you want your sauces to thicken, add flour or corn starch.
- Don't put too many ingredients in your slow cooker; fill it between one half and two thirds full.
- Trim any excess fats from meat; this will make your gravies and sauces silkier.
- If you are using wine among your ingredients, you only need to use a splash; alcohol doesn't evaporate because the cooker is sealed.

Do's and Don'ts

- *Do* brown your meat before placing it into the slow cooker to make sure that it reaches the temperature standards for food safety.
- *Do* wash the insert of your slow cooker with hot soapy water before using it.
- *Do* thaw frozen foods before adding them to the slow cooker. If you don't, it will increase the cooking time.
- *Do* spray the cooker insert with a non-stick cooking spray before you put any food in it. This will make cleanup a lot easier.
- *Do* add tender ingredients such as mushrooms, fish, zucchini and peas during the final 30 minutes to 1 hour of cooking. This will enable them to release their flavors without getting mushy because they have been over cooked.
- *Do* arrange the foods that take longer to cook at the bottom of the cooker.

- ☐ *Don't* use abrasive cleansers and sponges to clean the cooker insert or it will get scratched and damaged.
- ☐ *Don't* reheat meat leftovers in a slow cooker; the temperature won't get hot enough to heat the food to meat safety standards. Instead, use a microwave.
- ☐ *Don't* store leftovers in the slow cooker; transfer them into a container and store them in the fridge.
- ☐ *Don't* place the cooker insert over direct heat such as an electric or a gas burner; extreme or sudden temperature changes can cause it to break. For the same reason, don't put the insert in the freezer or the oven.
- ☐ *Don't* add dairy products until the final thirty minutes to one hour of cooking; when they are cooked too long on a high temperature, dairy products start curdling and separating.
- ☐ *Don't* preheat your slow cooker unless the recipe you are making requires you to.
- ☐ *Don't* place your slow cooker next to a draft or near an open window; this will cause the slow cooker not to reach its maximum temperature.
- ☐ *Don't* open the lid and stir your ingredients. Stirring isn't necessary because one of the advantages of using a slow cooker is that it prevents the food from sticking to the bottom.

Maintenance of a Slow Cooker

- ☐ Soak your slow cooker insert in soapy water for 2 hours before washing it. Make sure the tap water is at its hottest temperature.
- ☐ If you are still finding your slow cooker difficult to clean after soaking it for 2 hours, sprinkle 1/4 cup of baking soda into the slow cooker, add some dish soap, fill it with water and turn it on

high for 2 to 4 hours.
- ☐ When you are cooking with foods that burn easily. such as sugar and BBQ sauce. use a crock pot liner.
- ☐ Make sure your slow cooker is turned off when it is not in use.
- ☐ Do not use the glass lid or stoneware liner if it is severely scratched, chipped or cracked.
- ☐ For the removal of mineral deposits or water spots, use distilled white vinegar to wipe the liner down.
- ☐ Use a soft slightly damp sponge or cloth to wipe the exterior and the interior base.

OK! Now you must have already known about the slow cooker very much. Let's get into the recipe part. From now on, you will enjoy 123 fantastic recipes that you can make easily at home or anywhere by your slow cooker! We have a selection of **Meat Dishes, Poultry Dishes, Vegan & Vegetarian Dishes, Appetizers, Side Dishes, Desserts and Soups & Broths,** to give you meals that can be made ahead of time and waiting for you at any occasion!

Please be noted that these recipes are super simple, and all include 5 ingredients or less! Personal taste is very important, though, so salt and pepper have not been included in the ingredients list. It will be up to you to season to just how you like it! But we have included the salt, pepper, water, etc. on direction part. I think you will like these recipes! Enjoy!

Meat Dishes

1. Barbecue Pulled

Pork

Serves: 8

Preparation time: 35 minutes + 6 hours cooking time

Ingredients:

- 72 oz pork shoulder
- 1 onion
- 1 cup ketchup
- 1 tablespoon mustard
- 1/4 cup brown sugar

Direction:

1) Cut the pork shoulder up into 4 pieces, so that it will all fit into the slow cooker.
2) Peel and dice the onion, and mix it together with the ketchup, mustard and brown sugar, as well as ¼ of a cup of water. Season with salt and pepper.
3) Pour the ketchup mixture all over the pieces of pork in the slow cooker.
4) Cook on High for 6 hours, until the pork is nice and tender. Then, remove it from the cooker and use 2 forks to 'pull' or shred it.
5) Transfer the cooking liquid into a saucepan and bring it to the

boil to thicken and serve as a sauce.

Serving Suggestion: I love my perfect pulled pork served in a soft bread roll and with sweet potato fries!

Tip: If you like it hot, switch half of the ketchup out for chilli sauce and give it a good kick!

2. Sweet & Sour Brisket

Serves: 6

Preparation time: 30 minutes + 3 hours cooking time

Ingredients:

- ☐ 64 oz beef brisket
- ☐ 2-1/2 tablespoons red wine vinegar
- ☐ 2 onions
- ☐ 1/2 cup ketchup
- ☐ 1/2 cup brown sugar

Direction:

1) Season the brisket well with salt and pepper. Place it into a pan with a little oil for 10 minutes to begin browning. Turn it every few minutes to get an even cooking. Then, place it into your slow cooker.
2) Peel and dice the onion, and mix it together the with ketchup, red wine vinegar, brown sugar and 1/2 a cup of water. Season with salt and pepper.
3) Pour the mixture all over the brisket inside the slow cooker and cook on Low for 8 hours.
4) To make a sauce to serve with the brisket, add the cooking liquid into a pan and allow it to boil and thicken, seasoning with salt and pepper again to taste, if need be.

Serving Suggestion: For w arming winter dinner, serve with steamed veggies and smooth mashed potato, perfect for pouring the sauce all over!

Tip: The good news is that this brisket keeps really nicely for up to 2 days. So, you could cook this brisket overnight one day and then have it ready for serving the next day or the one after!

3. Mediterranean Lamb Shanks

Serves: 4
Preparation time: 30 minutes + 4 hours cooking time

Ingredients:

- ☐ 4 lamb shanks
- ☐ 4 sprigs dill
- ☐ 2 garlic cloves
- ☐ 1 lemon
- ☐ 1/2 cup feta cheese

Direction:

1) Rub salt and pepper into the lamb shanks to season them well.
2) Then, begin browning them in a pan, with a little oil, for about 10 minutes, turning them so that it's even.
3) Peel and thinly slice the garlic, and slice the lemon up into wedges.
4) Place the lamb shanks into the slow cooker and add in the garlic, lemon and dill, as well as 2/3 of a cup of salted water.
5) Cook on High for 3-1/2 - 4 hours, until the lamb is tender.
6) Sprinkle the feta on to the lamb shanks to serve.

Serving Suggestion: Keep it Mediterranean and serve with herby couscous and grilled eggplant – delicious!

Tip: You can make a little sauce with the cooking juices, seasoning with salt, pepper and lemon juice to your liking. Just skim the fat and then heat and reduce the juices in a pan.

4. Coconut Ribs

Serves: 6
Preparation time: 30 minutes + 5 hours cooking time

Ingredients:

- [ ] 56 oz pork ribs
- [ ] 14 fl oz coconut milk
- [ ] 2 garlic cloves
- [ ] 2 tablespoons lime juice
- [ ] 1-1/2 tablespoons ground cumin

Direction:

1) Trim any excess fat from the ribs.
2) Peel and dice the garlic, and soften it a little in a pan in a dash of the coconut milk.
3) Then, mix together the garlic, remaining coconut milk, lime juice and ground cumin, and season with salt and pepper to taste.
4) Pour the mixture all over the ribs in the slow cooker and cook on Low for 5 hours until tender.

Serving Suggestion: Keep this meal light and fresh by serving it with rice and a fresh cilantro, lime and chilli salad.

Tip: Take the cooking liquid and bring to the boil in a pan and then reduce it down to make a delicious dipping sauce.

5. Beer Braised Pot Roast

Serves: 8

Preparation time: 40 minutes + 8 hours cooking time

Ingredients:

- 64 oz braising beef
- 24 fl oz stout beer
- 3 tablespoons tomato puree
- 2 tablespoons instant coffee
- 2 tablespoons thyme

Direction:

1) Mix the instant coffee together with some salt and pepper and rub the mix all over your beef.
2) After letting it stand for 10 minutes, brown the beef on all sides in a pan.
3) Place the beef into the slow cooker, and reserve the fat in the pan.

4) Peel and mince the garlic into the fat, and stir in the tomato puree too. After a minute, whisk in the beer and thyme. Bring to the boil and then leave it reducing for about 15 minutes.
5) Pour the beer mixture all over the beef in the slow cooker and cook on Low for at least 8 hours, until the beef is deliciously tender.

Serving Suggestion: Add carrots, onions, potatoes and other veggies into the pot to cook along with the beef for more in your meal!

Tip: Reserve the cooking juices from the slow cooker and reduce them down to make a delicious gravy to serve alongside your roast.

6. Red Wine Beef Stew

Serves: 6
Preparation time: 20 minutes + 6 hours cooking time
Ingredients:

- ☐ 48 oz stewing beef

- ☐ 16 oz mushrooms
- ☐ 10 fl oz beef stock
- ☐ 1 onion
- ☐ 1 cup red wine

Direction:

1) Chop the beef up into chunks and it all into the slow cooker, along with the onion once it's been peeled and sliced.
2) Peel and halve the mushrooms and place them into the pot too.
3) Mix together the beef stock with the red wine, and season it well with salt and pepper.
4) Pour the mixture all over the beef in the slow cooker.
5) Cook on High for 6 hours until the beef is nice and tender.

Serving Suggestion: Well, the best thing for these rich, delicious juices has to be some form of carbohydrate, in my opinion! Take your pick of mashed potato, dumplings, fresh bread, spaghetti... the list is endless!

Tip: Just for the full experience, I think that the best way to make this dish is preparing it all in the morning and leaving it in the slow cooker, to be greeted by the rich aroma when you make it home after a long, cold day at work. Perfection

7. Java Roast Beef

Serves: 12
Preparation time: 20 minutes + 8 hours cooking time

Ingredients:

- ☐ 56 oz boneless beef chuck
- ☐ 5 garlic cloves
- ☐ 2 tablespoons cornstarch
- ☐ 1-1/2 cups strong coffee

Direction:

1) Mince the garlic and stir it together with a good amount of salt and pepper.
2) Rub the mixture all over the beef and place it into the slow cooker.
3) Pour the coffee in and cook on Low for 8 hours, until the meat is tender.
4) Once the meat is cooked, leave it to sit, and take the cooking juices and pour them into a saucepan. Mix in the cornstarch and 1/4 of a cup of water, whisking well until you have a nice, smooth sauce.

Serving Suggestion: The best way to do a good roast is with perfect roast potatoes and a tonne of vegetable sides!

Tip: If your meat isn't so tender after 8 hours, just keep it cooking until it is!

8. Apple & Garlic Roast Pork

Serves: 12
Preparation time: 20 minutes + 8 hours cooking time

Ingredients:

60 oz boneless pork loin
12 oz apple jelly
4 garlic cloves
1 tablespoon dried parsley

Direction:

1) If necessary, cut your roast in half to fit it all into the slow cooker.
2) Mince the garlic into a bowl, and stir in the apple jelly and parsley and season well with salt and pepper.
3) Pour the mixture all over the pork, and cook for 8 hours on Low.

Serving Suggestion: Nothing goes with this roast pork like garlic mashed potatoes!

Tip: Let your meat stand for 5 minutes or so before carving, otherwise the juices will run out and it won't look so appetizing on the plate.

9. Tater Tot Casserole

Serves: 4
Preparation time: 20 minutes + 8 hours cooking time

Ingredients:

☐ 16 oz ground beef

- ☐ 16 oz frozen tater tots
- ☐ 14 fl oz cream of chicken soup
- ☐ 2 cups cheese
- ☐ 1 onion

Direction:

1) In a pan, begin browning the ground beef.
2) Peel and dice the onion and stir it in with the beef.
3) Add the beef mixture into the slow cooker and pour in the cream of chicken soup.
4) Place the tater tots in a layer on top of the beef and cook on Low for 2 hours.
5) Then, sprinkle the cheese all over the top and cook for another 30 minutes.

Serving Suggestion: Steamed veggies in the winter or salad in the summer!

Tip: If you don't have tater tots... or feel too grown up for them(!), you can simply slice up potatoes and layer them on top

10. Barbacoa

Serves: 8
Preparation time: 20 minutes + 7 hours cooking time
Ingredients:

- ☐ 24 fl oz fl oz red wine

- ☐ 10 garlic cloves
- ☐ 4 dried chillies
- ☐ 3-1/2 oz dark chocolate
- ☐ 1 lamb shoulder

Direction:

1) Soak the chillies in boiling water for 2 minutes. Then, you can slice them open and remove the seeds.
2) Peel the garlic and blitz it up with the chillies and a pinch of salt and pepper and 1/3 of the wine.
3) Place the lamb shoulder into the slow cooker, and pour the wine and chilli mixture over the top.
4) Crumble the chocolate in, and pour in the remaining wine.
5) Cook on Low for 7 hours.

Serving Suggestion:
Reduce the wine and cooking liquids down to make a nice sauce, and serve with new potatoes in the summer, or mash in the winter.

Tip:
If your slow cooker isn't big enough for the full shoulder, you can slice it in half and layer the two pieces on top, or cook in 2 batches for a meal on 2 different days!

11. Ginger Ham

Serves: 8

Preparation time: 10 minutes + 7 hours cooking time

Ingredients:

- ☐ 50 fl oz ginger beer
- ☐ 10 cloves
- ☐ 1 onion
- ☐ 1 ham joint

Direction:

1) Peel the onion and slice it thickly. Toss it together with the cloves and put them into the bottom of the slow cooker.
2) Place the ham in.
3) Pour in the ginger beer, and add a good sprinkling of salt and pepper.
4) Cook on Low for 7 hours.

Serving Suggestion: A nice, fresh cabbage slaw goes perfectly well.

Tip: To get a nice sticky glaze on your ham, try this; remove the skin from the ham, leaving a small layer of fat, and score it diagonally. Stud in another 10 cloves. Mix together 1 tablespoon of English mustard with 3 tablespoons of ginger preserve and brush it all over the top of the ham. Bake for 20 minutes.

12. Irish Stew

Serves: 6

Preparation time: 10 minutes + 7 hours cooking time

Ingredients:

- ☐ 32 oz stewing lamb
- ☐ 7 oz streaky bacon
- ☐ 3 onions
- ☐ 3 oz pearl barley
- ☐ 1 sprig thyme

Direction:

1) Slice up the bacon and fry it in a pan until crispy. Then, pour the bacon bits into the slow cooker, and brown the lamb in the pan.
2) Add the lamb into the slow cooker too, along with the thyme.
3) Peel and slice the onions and add them into the slow cooker.
4) Pour in 23 fl oz of water and season well with salt and pepper.
5) Cook on Low for 7 hours. Then, stir in the pearl barley and season again to taste.
6) Cook for another hour on High and then enjoy!

Serving Suggestion: Either serve with oven roasted veggies, or just add all the veggies into the slow cooker for a great one pot meal!

Tip: Remember to remove the thyme sprig before serving. It's great as an infused flavour, but you don't want to bite down into that!

13. Sticky Lamb Shanks

Serves: 2
Preparation time: 15 minutes + 6 hours cooking time

Ingredients:

- ☐ 14 oz canned tomatoes
- ☐ 4 dried apricots
- ☐ 3 onions
- ☐ 2 lamb shanks
- ☐ 2 tablespoons pomegranate molasses

Direction:

1) Season the lamb shanks with salt and pepper, and begin browning them for 5 minutes in a pan.
2) Peel and slice up the onions and add them into the pan too, to soften.
3) Add the shanks and onions to the slow cooker, and brush on the molasses. Gently pour in the canned tomatoes.
4) Chop up the dried apricots and sprinkle them in.
5) Pour in water until just the top of the lamb shanks are out above it, so that the glaze doesn't get washed off!
6) Cook on High for 6 hours.

Serving Suggestion: Rice with fresh cilantro makes a fresh side.

Tip: This makes a great 'meal for two'. To give it that special presentation factor, you can 'French' the bones. This means scraping the bone sticking out of the shank clean so that it looks extra nice.

14. Herby Sausage Casserole

Serves: 4

Preparation time: 10 minutes + 2 hours cooking time

Ingredients:

- [ ] 30 oz canned beans of your choice
- [ ] 28 oz canned tomatoes
- [ ] 8-12 sausages
- [ ] 2 teaspoons dried oregano
- [ ] 1 teaspoon dried basil

Direction:

1) Place the sausages in a pan to begin browning for 5 minutes or so. Then, place them into the slow cooker.
2) Drain the beans and add them into the slow cooker too, as well as the canned tomatoes and the dried oregano and basil.
3) Stir everything together, and season with salt and pepper to taste. Cook on High for 2 hours.

Serving Suggestion: What could be better than sausage and mash?!

Tip: You can get sausages of so many different flavours, so pick something that will really compliment this sauce well, like pork and apple for example.

15. Goan Pulled Pork

Serves: 4

Preparation time: 25 minutes + 8 hours cooking time

Ingredients:

- ☐ 70 oz pork shoulder
- ☐ 10 garlic cloves
- ☐ 7-1/2 fl oz cider vinegar
- ☐ 3 inches ginger
- ☐ 1 tablespoon ground cumin

Direction:

1) Peel and mince the ginger and garlic, and add them into a frying pan to become fragrant.
2) Then, stir in the cumin and vinegar.
3) Place the pork shoulder into the slow cooker, and pour the vinegar mixture all over it,
4) Season well with salt and pepper, and cook on Low for 8 hours.
5) When the pork is cooked, remove the rind and fat.
6) Shred the meat with 2 forks.

Serving Suggestion: Chipatis and the fresh salad found in tips is the way to make this into a meal!

Tip: Shred 3 carrots and a red onion, and mix together with 2 diced tomatoes and a handful of fresh coriander. Season with lemon juice and olive oil.

16. Beef Lo Mein

Serves: 4

Preparation time: 25 minutes + 8 hours cooking time

Ingredients:

- ☐ 32 oz chuck steak
- ☐ 16 oz frozen vegetables
- ☐ 12 oz stir fry sauce (recipe in tips)
- ☐ 12 oz lo mein noodles
- ☐ 8 oz canned water chestnuts

Direction:

1) Trim off any fat from the meat, and chop it up into 1 inch cubes. Add the beef into a pan to begin browning.
2) Add the meat into the slow cooker, along with the chestnuts and their liquid, and the stir fry sauce.
3) Season with salt and pepper to taste.
4) Cook on Low for 7 hours, and then add in the frozen vegetables. Cook on High for another 30-60 minutes.
5) Meanwhile, cook the noodles according to the package instructions.
6) Stir the noodles through the meat and sauce and serve hot.

Serving Suggestion: give yourself the 'take out experience' by grabbing a bag iof prawn crackers to go along with this.

Tip: For a super simple stir fry sauce, combine together 2 tablespoons of brown sugar in a pan with 1/3 of a cup of soy sauce. Whilst it's simmering, stir 2 tablespoons of cornstarch together with

2 tablespoons of boiling water. Stir the cornstarch mixture into the sauce to thicken at the end.

17. Pork Cutlets with Apple

Serves: 4

Preparation time: 20 minutes + 3-1/2 hours cooking time

Ingredients:

- 4 pork cutlets
- 2 apples
- 2 garlic cloves
- 1-1/2 tablespoons English mustard
- 1 cup white wine

Direction:

1) Trim off excess fat off of the pork cutlets and season them with salt and pepper.
2) Sear the cutlets for 2 minutes on each side in a pan, and then place them into the slow cooker.
3) Core, peel and slice the apple, and stir it around in the pan for 2-3 minutes, before adding it into the pan too.
4) Stir the mustard into the white wine, and pour the mixture all over the pork and apples.
5) Mince the garlic cloves into the slow cooker too, and stir everything around.
6) Cook on High for 3-1/2 hours.

Serving Suggestion: Roasted parsnips and steamed greens are the way to finish off this meal!

Tip: Do be aware of the sweetness of the apples you use! Green cooking apples may be the best if you don't like a lot of sweetness. If you do, then Pink Ladies may be a nice choice.

18. Beef & Ale Stew

Serves: 4

Preparation time: 20 minutes + 7 hours cooking time

Ingredients:

- [ ] 50 oz stewing steak
- [ ] 14-3/4 fl oz dark ale or stout
- [ ] 14 fl oz beef stock
- [ ] 12 shallots
- [ ] 2 tablespoons tomato paste

Direction:

1) Chop the steak up into 1 inch cubes, and add it into a pan to brown all over.
2) Peel and slice the shallots, and soften them in the pan for 3 minutes.
3) Add the steak and shallots into the slow cooker, and pout in the ale and beef stock.
4) Stir in the tomato paste and season well with salt and pepper. Cook on Low for 7 hours.

Serving Suggestion: Potatoes of some sort, of course! Take your pick of roasted, mashed or wedges!

Tip: If you like, add vegetables into the slow cooker too, and get some more goodness into this meal!

19. Tunisian Spiced Lamb

Serves: 4

Preparation time: 15 minutes + 6 hours cooking time

Ingredients:

- ☐ 6 lamb shanks
- ☐ 2 teaspoons ground cumin
- ☐ 2 teaspoons ground coriander seeds
- ☐ 2 cinnamon sticks
- ☐ 1/2 cup fresh mint

Direction:

1) Mix together the cumin and coriander seeds with some salt and pepper, and rub it all over the lamb shanks.
2) Place the lamb shanks into a pan to brown all over for 2-3 minutes.
3) Add the lamb into the slow cooker, and place in the cinnamon sticks.
4) Pour in 4 cups of water, and season well with salt and pepper.
5) Cook on High for 6 hours, and serve with the fresh mint sprinkled on the lamb.

Serving Suggestion: Minty couscous is the perfect side dish to this!

Tip: A great way to get more flavour into any dish is by using stocks. If you like, replace the water with lamb or vegetable stock for that little bit extra.

20. Pork Belly

Serves: 4

Preparation time: 20 minutes + 7 hours cooking time

Ingredients:

17-1/2 oz pork belly
1 garlic clove
1 tablespoon soy sauce
1 tablespoon honey
1 tablespoon sherry

Direction:

1) Slice the pork belly up into rashers and pat them dry with a paper towel.
2) Mince the garlic and mix it together with the soy sauce, honey and sherry. Pour the mixture into the slow cooker.
3) Layer the pork rashers over the top of the sauce.
4) Cook on Low for 7 hours.

Serving Suggestion: A barbecue dipping sauce would do wonders!

Tip: If you like, place the rashers skin side down in a pan once they're cooked to get a nice bit of crispiness on the skin.

Poultry Dishes

1. Incredibly Garlicky Chicken

Serves: 6

Preparation time: 30 minutes + 3 hours cooking time

Ingredients:

- ☐ 3 whole garlic bulbs (around 30+ cloves)
- ☐ 12 skinless chicken pieces
- ☐ 2/3 cup olives
- ☐ 1/2 cup dry white wine
- ☐ 1/2 tablespoon saffron

Direction:

1) Break the saffron up into small pieces whilst mixing it into the white wine.
2) Season the chicken pieces with salt and pepper, and then rub the white wine mixture into the chicken pieces.
3) Into the slow cooker, add the chicken, any leftover white wine and 2-1/2 cups water, well seasoned with salt and pepper.
4) Separate the garlic heads into cloves, but leave them unpeeled. Spread the cloves out amongst the chicken in the cooker.
5) Cook on High for 2-1/2 hours.
6) Slice up the olives and add them to the cooker, cooking for another 15-20 minutes before serving.

Serving Suggestion: Some toasted fresh ciabatta bread is perfect for soaking up those delicious, garlicky stew juices!

Tip: For added nutritional value, chop up veggies and have them cooking in the stew too. Leeks, celery, onions and carrots all work wonderfully.

2. Honey Apricot Chicken

Serves: 4

Preparation time: 20 minutes + 3-1/4 hours cooking time

Ingredients:

- [ ] 8 skinless chicken thighs
- [ ] 2 tablespoons mustard
- [ ] 1 onion
- [ ] 1/4 cup apricot brandy
- [ ] 1/4 cup honey

Direction:

1) Season the chicken pieces with salt and pepper, and begin browning them in a pan, for about 3 minutes on each side. Then, remove the chicken from the pan and place it into the slow cooker.
2) Peel and chop the onion and add it into the pan, along with the apricot brandy to soften.
3) One the onion is softened, add it into the slow cooker with the chicken.
4) Whisk together the honey and mustard with 1/2 a cup of

seasoned water.
5) Pour the mixture into the slow cooker and cook on Low for 4 hours until the chicken is tender.

Serving Suggestion: Make a nice sauce with the cooking liquid and 2 tablespoons of butter. Reduce it down and re-season in a pan. Then, serve on a bed of rice for a simple but super tasty dinner.

Tip: If you like the skin and decide to keep it on, make sure that it really gets crisped up in the pan before placing it into the slow cooker, otherwise the texture of it really won't be nice.

3. BBQ Whole Chicken

Serves: 6

Preparation time: 20 minutes + 5 hours cooking time

Ingredients:

- 2 tablespoons Bourbon whiskey
- 1-1/2 teaspoons paprika
- 1 whole chicken
- 1/2 cup cola
- 1/4 cup ketchup

Direction:

1) Mix the paprika together with a good amount of salt and pepper, and rub it all over the chicken. Then, place the chicken into the slow cooker.

2) Mix together the cola, ketchup and Bourbon and pour the mixture all over the chicken, ensuring to get it into the crevices too.
3) Cook on High for 5 hours.

Serving Suggestion: Make a light, summery dinner by shredding the chicken and filling a sub roll with it. Fill up with lettuce, cucumber, tomato, mayonnaise, barbecue sauce, jalapenos and finally drizzle on the cooking juices from the slow cooker – it's heavenly!

Tip: If you have a smaller slow cooker, you can chop the chicken up into pieces first and fit them into the slow cooker that way.

4. Cashew Chicken

Serves: 6
Preparation time: 20 minutes + 4 hours cooking time

Ingredients:

- ☐ 32 oz skinless, boneless chicken
- ☐ 4 tablespoons sweet chilli sauce
- ☐ 2 garlic cloves
- ☐ 1 cup cashews
- ☐ 1/2 cup soy sauce

Direction:

1) Chop the chicken into bite sized pieces. Begin browning it in a pan for 2-3 minutes.
2) Mix the soy sauce together with the sweet chilli sauce.
3) Peel and mince the garlic and stir it into the soy sauce mixture. Stir the cashews through it too.
4) Place the chicken into the slow cooker and pour the cashew mixture all over it.
5) Cook on Low for 3-4 hours, until the chicken is tender.

Serving Suggestion: Rice or noodles!

Tip: Using low sodium soy sauce is a good idea, if you can get hold of it. Obviously, less salt is better for you, and it makes it less likely that the dish gets too salty.

5. Cheesy Chicken Taquitos

Makes: 12

Preparation time: 5 minutes + 4-1/4 hours cooking time

Ingredients:

- ☐ 12 tortillas
- ☐ 8 oz cream cheese
- ☐ 2 boneless, skinless chicken breasts
- ☐ 1-1/2 teaspoons chilli powder
- ☐ 1 teaspoon cumin

Direction:

1) Into the slow cooker, add the chicken, chilli powder, cumin, cream cheese and 1/3 of a cup of water. Cook on High for 4 hours.
2) Remove the chicken from the slow cooker and sue 2 forks to shred it. Place it back into the cooker.
3) Stir everything well together and cook for another 15 minutes.
4) Meanwhile, have the oven preheating to 400F.
5) Into each tortilla, add 2 tablespoons of the chicken mixture, in the centre.
6) Roll the tortillas up into tubes, and place them, fold side down onto a baking tray lined with parchment paper.
7) Bake for 10 minutes until the tortillas are nicely browned and crunchy.

Serving Suggestion: Make a bar of toppings such as guacamole, Mexican shredded cheese, sour cream, green onions, jalapenos etc and let everyone dress their own!

Tip : Although possibly less traditional, wheat tortillas tend to work better than corn tortillas for this kind of dish.

6. Balsamic Chicken Lettuce Cups

Serves: 4

Preparation time: 15 minutes + 3 1/2 hours cooking time

Ingredients:

- 24 oz skinless, boneless chicken
- 2 garlic cloves
- 1 Boston lettuce
- 1 tablespoons fresh ginger
- 1/4 cup balsamic vinegar

Direction:

1) Peel and mince the ginger and garlic into the slow cooker, and mix in the balsamic vinegar.
2) Place the chicken into the cooker too, and stir around to coat it in the sauce.
3) Cook on High for 3-1/2 hours.
4) When the chicken is cooked, sue 2 forks to shred it.
5) Use large lettuce leaves to crate cups in your hand, and fill them with spoonfuls of the chicken mixture.

Serving Suggestion: Take this from a snack into a filling dinner by also filling the lettuce sups with rice.

Tip: Add in some spice if you like it hot!

7. Maple & Mustard Chicken

Serves: 6
Preparation time: 5 minutes + 3 hours cooking time

Ingredients:

- ☐ 6 skinless, boneless chicken breasts
- ☐ 2 tablespoons tapioca
- ☐ 1/2 cup maple syrup
- ☐ 1/3 cup mustard

Direction:

1) Place your chicken into the slow cooker.
2) Mix together the tapioca, maple syrup and mustard, and then pour the mixture all over the chicken.
3) Cook on Low for 3 hours.

Serving Suggestion: This chicken is so flavoursome that simple brown rice and fresh green onions is all you'll need to make this into a delicious meal!

Tip: Adapt this into more of a roast by using a whole chicken instead.

8. Teriyaki

Chicken

Serves: 4

Preparation time: 5 minutes + 3 hours cooking time

Ingredients:

- [ ] 24 oz skinless, boneless chicken breasts
- [ ] 3 garlic cloves
- [ ] 1/2 cup soy sauce
- [ ] 1/4 cup honey
- [ ] 1/4 cup brown sugar

Direction:

1) Chop the chicken up into small pieces and add it into the slow cooker.
2) Mince the garlic cloves and mix them together with the soy sauce, honey and brown sugar.
3) Pour the mixture all over the chicken.
4) Cook on High for 4 hours.
5) If your sauce isn't thick enough, you can add it into a saucepan after removing the chicken, and bring it to the boil to thicken up.

Serving Suggestion: Serve on a bed of brown rice and sprinkle with sesame seeds and chopped green onions.

Tip: This is the perfect freezer meal! It freezes so well and then you can simply thaw it and re-heat in the microwave for delicious food another day too!

9. Creamy Herby Italian

Chicken

Serves: 4

Preparation time: 5 minutes + 3-1/2 hours cooking time

Ingredients:

- [ ] 14 fl oz cream of chicken soup
- [ ] 8 oz cream cheese
- [ ] 4 boneless, skinless chicken breasts
- [ ] 2 teaspoons dried oregano
- [ ] 1 cup fresh basil

Direction:

1) Place the chicken into the slow cooker, and sprinkle on the dried oregano. Also add a good dash of salt and pepper.
2) Pour in the cream of chicken soup.
3) Chop the cream cheese up into cubes and add it into the pot.
4) Add in the basil, and cook on High for 3-1/2 hours.

Serving Suggestion: Serve with spaghetti and a green salad.

Tip: You can also cook this on Low for 7-8 hours. This is great if you want to stick it on in the morning and have something ready for you when you get home from work!

10. Duck with Orange

Serves: 4

Preparation time: 10 minutes + 8 hours cooking time

Ingredients:

- ☐ 70 oz duck
- ☐ 2 bay leaves
- ☐ 2 tablespoons honey
- ☐ 1 onion
- ☐ 3/4 cup orange juice

Direction:

1) Season the duck all over with salt and pepper.
2) Add a little oil into a pan and begin browning the duck all over on all sides.
3) Remove the duck and allow any fat to drain off.
4) Peel and slice the onion and add it into the slow cooker, along with the bay leaves.
5) Mix together the orange juice and honey and pour into the slow cooker.
6) Place the duck into the slow cooker and cook on Low for 8 hours.

Serving Suggestion: Chinese style on a bed of egg fried rice is perfect.

Tip: You can make a nice sticky sauce by thickening up the cooking juices with some corn starch in a pan.

11. Sweet & Sour Chicken

Serves: 4

Preparation time: 10 minutes + 8 hours cooking time

Ingredients:

- ☐ 14 oz canned pineapple chunks
- ☐ 4 skinless, boneless chicken breasts
- ☐ 3 tablespoons sweet chilli sauce
- ☐ 2 teaspoons minced garlic
- ☐ 1 red bell pepper

Direction:

1) Chop up the chicken and de-seed and chop up the red bell pepper.
2) Add them both into the slow cooker, along with the pineapple, after draining it.
3) Mince the garlic and mix it together with the sweet chilli sauce, 1 cup of water and a pinch of salt.
4) Pour the sauce into the slow cooker and stir it around to cover the ingredients.
5) Cook on High for 2-1/2 hours.

Serving Suggestion: Make this your perfect 'Chinese take-out at home' by serving with vegetable fried rice, and maybe some sneaky spring rolls on the side!

Tip: To thicken up your sauce, if you like it that way, mix 3 tablespoons of corn starch together with 4 tablespoons of water. Stir it into the dish about 30 minutes before the cooking time is up.

12. Turkey Meatballs

Serves: 6

Preparation time: 30 minutes + 6 hours cooking time

Ingredients:

- ☐ 32 oz lean ground turkey
- ☐ 28 oz canned tomatoes
- ☐ 2 teaspoons basil
- ☐ 1 egg
- ☐ 2/3 cup cooked quinoa

Direction:

1) In a bowl, combine the ground turkey, basil, egg and cooked quinoa, as well as a good pinch of salt and pepper.
2) Roll the ground turkey mix into balls, slightly smaller than golf balls, and add them into a pan to begin browning on the outside.
3) Pour half of the canned tomatoes into the bottom of the slow cooker, and then add in the meatballs. Top with the remaining half of the tomatoes and season with a pinch of salt and pepper on top.
4) Cook on Low for 6 hours.

Serving Suggestion: Serve with spaghetti for a delightful Italian-inspired dinner.

Tip: To get even more flavour into this dish, cook your quinoa in a really flavoursome and herby broth.

13. Chicken Pesto Pasta

Serves: 8

Preparation time: 10 minutes + 5-1/4 hours cooking time

Ingredients:

- [ ] 16 oz pasta
- [ ] 8 skinless, boneless chicken breasts
- [ ] 2 cups mozzarella
- [ ] 1 cup pesto (recipe in tips if you want to make your own)
- [ ] 1/2 cup fresh basil to garnish

Direction:

1) Slice up the chicken and season with salt and pepper. Add it into the slow cooker.
2) Pour on the pesto and cook on Low for 5 hours.
3) Cook the pasta according to the package instructions and stir it into the chicken and pesto.
4) Shred the mozzarella and sprinkle it on top of the pasta. Tear the basil and sprinkle it on.
5) Cook for a further 15 minutes until the mozzarella is melted, and then enjoy!

Serving Suggestion: Warm ciabatta from the oven is a delicious accompaniment. A green salad is a great idea to get some extra vitamins too.

Tip: To make your own pesto, you simply need to blitz together a green leaf (spinach, basil etc), a nut (usually pine nuts, but you could use cashews or something else), an oil (olive oil usually), garlic and dried parmesan.

14. Spanish Chicken

Serves: 6

Preparation time: 15 minutes + 6 hours cooking time

Ingredients:

- [ ] 12 bone-in chicken thighs
- [ ] 10 fl oz white wine
- [ ] 8 oz chorizo
- [ ] 5-1/2 oz green olives
- [ ] 3 bell peppers of any colour

Direction:

1) Slice up the chorizo and place it into a pan along with the chicken thighs for a few minutes to begin browning all over.
2) Meanwhile, you can de-seed and slice up the bell peppers, and slice up the olives.
3) Then, add the vegetables and meat all into the slow cooker, and

pour in the white wine.
4) Pour in another 10 fl oz of water, and season well with salt and pepper.
5) Cook on Low for 6 hours.

Serving Suggestion: Spanish saffron rice is the best side for this dish!

Tip: Dry white wine works best. The peppers, depending on which colours you choose, can be pretty sweet by themselves, so a dry white wine will round out the flavour better.

15. Festive Turkey

Serves: 4

Preparation time: 20 minutes + 3-1/2 hours cooking time

Ingredients:

- 16 rashers smoked bacon
- 5 fl oz white wine
- 5 cups vegetables of your choice
- 2 large turkey breasts
- 2 tablespoons fresh thyme

Direction:

1) Wrap 8 rashers of bacon around each turkey breast.
2) Rub some black pepper into the bacon wrapped turkey.
3) Begin crisping up the bacon in a pan for 5 minutes or so.
4) Prepare the vegetables you have chosen, and add them into

the bottom of the slow cooker, seasoning well with salt and pepper. Chop up the thyme and sprinkle it in.
5) Layer the turkey breasts on top, and pour in the white wine.
6) Also, add in 17 fl oz of well seasoned water, and then cook on Low for 3-1/2 hours.

Serving Suggestion: The way to do this kind of dinner is with potatoes of your choice, and as many veggies as you can pile up, am I right?

Tip: Strain the cooking juices and thicken them up in a pan with a little flour to make your own gravy too.

16. Duck & Pineapple Curry

Serves: 6
Preparation time: 20 minutes + 6 hours cooking time

Ingredients:

- 14 fl oz coconut milk
- 6 duck legs
- 4 tablespoons red curry paste (recipe in tips)
- 2 tablespoons fish sauce
- 1 small pineapple

Direction:

1) Peel, core and chop the pineapple up into chunks and add it into the slow cooker.
2) Add in the duck legs, and pour in the coconut milk too.

3) Stir in the fish sauce and curry paste, and season with salt and pepper to taste.
4) Cook on Low for 6 hours.

Serving Suggestion: Make this Thai by squeezing lime juice and tearing fresh basil leaves.

Tip: To make red curry paste, toast in a pan cumin seeds, coriander seeds and black peppercorns until fragrant. Then, blitz them up into a powder. Add in 10 large dried chillies that have been soaked, galangal, lemongrass, coriander roots, shallots, garlic and shrimp paste. Blitz everything together until smooth and to your personal taste.

17. Chicken Adobo

Serves: 4-6

Preparation time: 20 minutes + 8 hours cooking time

Ingredients:

48 oz skinless bone-in chicken thighs
10 garlic cloves
3-1/2 fl oz soy sauce
2 onions
1 inch fresh ginger

Direction:

1) Season the chicken all over with pepper and place it into a pan to begin browning for a few minutes.
2) Drip off as much of the fat as possible and place the chicken

into the slow cooker.
3) Peel and slice up the onions and garlic and add them in too.
4) Grate the ginger in, and pour in the soy sauce.
5) Add in about 4 fl oz water too.
6) Season to taste, and then cook on Low for 8 hours.

Serving Suggestion: This traditional Filipino dish is perfect on a bed of brown rice and with steamed Asian greens.

Tip: Flabby skin is never really a good thing, so make sure to really crisp it up first in the pan!

18. Mango Jerk Chicken

Serves: 4

Preparation time: 20 minutes + 5 hours cooking time

Ingredients:

- 4 skinless, boneless chicken breasts
- 2 teaspoons jerk seasoning (recipe in tips)
- 1 mango
- 1 red onion
- 1/2 cup fresh cilantro

Direction:

1) Season the chicken breasts with salt and pepper.
2) Rub the jerk seasoning all over the chicken too and place it into the slow cooker with 4 tablespoons of water
3) Peel and slice up the mango and red onion and add them to the

slow cooker too.
4) Tear in the cilantro, and cook on Low for 5 hours.

Serving Suggestion: Serve with rice and beans to keep the Caribbean style going!

Tip: To make your own jerk seasoning, combine garlic powder, onion powder, brown sugar, thyme, parsley, paprika, allspice, cinnamon, nutmeg, curry powder, cayenne powder and chilli flakes. Blitz up into a powder, and store ay you don't use in an airtight jar.

19. Merlot Chicken

Serves: 4

Preparation time: 20 minutes + 3-1/2 hours cooking time

Ingredients:

- [ ] 4 skinless, boneless chicken breasts
- [ ] 3 cups mushrooms
- [ ] 2 tablespoons basil
- [ ] 1 onion
- [ ] 1/3 cup Merlot or other dry red wine

Direction:

1. Peel and slice up the onions and mushrooms and add them into the slow cooker.
2. Rub salt and pepper into the chicken breasts and sit them on top of the vegetables.
3. Mix the wine together with another 1/3 of a cup of water and

the basil, and pour it all over the chicken.
4. Cook on high for 3-1/2 hours.

Serving Suggestion: Serve this on a bad of creamy mash for a winter warming dinner!

Tip: You can add in more vegetables too to get all the extra goodness into this meal!

20. Peking Duck

Serves: 8

Preparation time: 20 minutes + 4 hours cooking time

Ingredients:

2 teaspoons Chinese 5 spice (recipe in tips)
1 bunch fresh green onions
1 whole duck
1/4 cup honey
1/4 cup soy sauce

Direction:

1) Pull back the duck skin, keeping it attached at the end.
2) Stir the Chinese 5 spice through the honey and rub it all under the skin. Pull the skin back over.
3) Rub salt and pepper into the suck sin.
4) Trim the green onions, and spread them out in the bottom of the slow cooker.
5) Place the duck on top and drizzle the soy sauce over the top.
6) Cook on High for 4 hours.

Serving Suggestion: Shred the duck and serve in pancakes with hoisin sauce!

Tip: If you're wondering what exactly are the 5 spices, try combining cinnamon, star anise, fennel seed, Szechuan pepper and cloves.

Seafood Dishes

1. Shrimp Jambalaya

Serves: 8

Preparation time: 20 minutes + 4 hours cooking time

Ingredients:

- ☐ 32 oz shrimp
- ☐ 14 oz canned tomatoes
- ☐ 4 garlic cloves
- ☐ 3 cups rice
- ☐ 2 tablespoons Creole seasoning (recipe in Tip)

Direction:

1) Peel and mince the garlic, and add it to the slow cooker, along with the tomatoes, Creole seasoning, a good pinch of salt and pepper and the rice.
2) Add in 6 cups of lightly salted water and cover the pot. Leave it cooking on High for 90 minutes.
3) Meanwhile, ensure that the shrimp are peeled and de-veined.
4) Add the shrimp into the slow cooker and cook on High for a further 15 minutes or so, until the shrimp are pinked and cooked through.

Serving Suggestion: For a more rounded out meal that needs nothing else, add vegetables into your jambalaya. The traditional choices are celery, green bell pepper and onion, but you can really add what you like! A sprinkle of fresh parsley to serve is always nice too.

Tip: For Creole seasoning, you can process together into a powder paprika, garlic powder, black pepper, onion powder, cayenne pepper, dried oregano and dried thyme. Adjust the quantities to your taste.

2. Poached Salmon

Serves: 4

Preparation time: 20 minutes + 4 hours cooking time

Ingredients:

- 4 salmon fillets
- 1 onion
- 1 sprig of fresh dill
- 1/2 cup dry white wine
- 1/4 of a lemon

Direction:

1) Into the slow cooker, add the wine and 1 cup of water.
2) Peel and dice the onion and add it into the slow cooker along with the lemon and dill. Season well with salt and pepper. Cook on High for 20 minutes.
3) Then, add in the salmon fillets and cook for a further 20 minutes, until the salmon is flaky and opaque.

Serving Suggestion: If it's warm and you're looking for a refreshing and light dinner, flake up the salmon and have it as part of a light, herby salad.

Tip: Try not to overcook the salmon! It may be worth checking it after 15 minutes to avoid that.

3. Garlic Shrimp

Serves: 4

Preparation time: 15 minutes + 1 hour cooking time

Ingredients:

- 24 oz jumbo shrimp
- 6 garlic cloves
- 2 tablespoons fresh parsley
- 1 teaspoon Creole seasoning
- 1/4 cup olive oil

Direction:

1) Peel and slice up the garlic, and add it into the slow cooker along with the olive oil and Creole seasoning. Cook on High for 25 minutes.
2) Meanwhile, if necessary, peel and de-vein your shrimp.
3) Add the shrimp into the slow cooker and stir to coat it in the olive oil mixture.
4) Cook on High for 15 minutes, give it a stir and then cook for another 15 minutes.
5) Chop up the fresh parsley and stir it in for just 1 minute at the end before serving.

Serving Suggestion: Go Southern and serve this on a bed of slow cooker cheese grits!

Tip: If you want to try your hand at your own Creole seasoning, mix paprika, salt, garlic powder, black pepper, onion powder, cayenne, oregano and thyme together to your taste.

4. Maple Salmon

Serves: 6

Preparation time: 5 minutes + 1 hour cooking time

Ingredients:

- 6 skinless salmon fillets
- 2 tablespoons lime juice
- 1 teaspoon minced ginger
- 1/2 cup maple syrup
- 1/4 cup soy sauce

Direction:

1) Place the salmon fillets into the slow cooker.
2) Mix together the lime juice, minced ginger, maple syrup and soy sauce, and pour it all over the salmon.
3) Cook on High for 1 hour.

Serving Suggestion: You can refrigerate this salmon and crumble it up in a salad, for a tasty and easy to take with you lunch.

Tip: Frozen fish can sometimes be cheaper. So, if you have frozen salmon fillets, use them and just increase the cooking time to 2 hours. Simples!

5. Cod Red Curry

Serves: 4

Preparation time: 15 minutes + 2 hours cooking time

Ingredients:

- ☐ 30 fl oz coconut milk
- ☐ 16 oz cod fillet
- ☐ 12 oz carrots
- ☐ 3-1/2 tablespoons red curry paste (recipe in tips)
- ☐ 1 red bell pepper

Direction:

1) Peel and julienne the carrots (chop them into matchsticks!)
2) De-seed and slice up the red bell pepper too.
3) Pour the coconut milk into the slow cooker, and whisk the curry paste into it. Season with salt and pepper to taste.
4) Stir in the red bell pepper and carrot sticks, and then place the cod on top of the mixture.
5) Cook on Low for 2 hours and crumble up the cod into small pieces before serving.

Serving Suggestion: Curry has to be with rice, doesn't it?

Tip: If you want to make your own red curry paste, try this; take 10 dried chillies and leave them to soak in warm water for 20 minutes, and then finely chop them. Then, add 1 teaspoon of cumin seeds, 2 teaspoons of coriander seeds and 1/2 a teaspoon of black peppercorns into a pan to toast and begin to become fragrant. Then, once they're cooled, grind them up into a powder, and mix them together with the chopped chillies, 1 stalk of chopped lemongrass (the white part only), 1 teaspoon of minced ginger, 6 finely chopped coriander roots, 2 finely chopped shallots, 4 chopped cloves of garlic, 2 teaspoons of shrimp paste or fish sauce, and an additional 8 chopped chillies. Blend the mixture with 1/4 of a cup of water until smooth. The leftover paste can be frozen!

6. Salmon & Spinach Spaghetti

Serves: 2

Preparation time: 20 minutes + 3-1/2 hours cooking time

Ingredients:

- ☐ 16 oz skinless salmon fillets
- ☐ 4 oz uncooked spaghetti
- ☐ 3 garlic cloves
- ☐ 2 cups spinach
- ☐ 2 cups chicken broth

Direction:

1) Pour the chicken broth into the slow cooker, and mince in the garlic. Also, stir in the spinach and season well with salt and pepper, to taste.
2) Cook for 2 hours on Low.
3) Cook the spaghetti according to the package instructions and add it into the slow cooker for an additional 1 and a half hours, along with the salmon.

Serving Suggestion: If you like it spicy, try making your own chilli oil and having a little drizzle over your pasta. It's perfect, trust me!

Tip: If you want to make this a little more 'gourmet', I find that linguine always adds that little something special. We chose spaghetti or the recipe though, to make it moe useful for everyday.

7. Coconut Shrimp Curry

Serves: 4
Preparation time: 15 minutes + 2-1/2 hours cooking time

Ingredients:

- [ ] 30 fl oz coconut milk
- [ ] 16 oz shrimp
- [ ] 5 lemons
- [ ] 4 garlic cloves
- [ ] 2 tablespoons red curry paste

Direction:

1) Zest the lemons and add it into the slow cooker.
2) Also, mine in the garlic, and stir in the coconut milk and curry paste. Taste, and season with salt and pepper to your liking.
3) Cook on High for 2 hours, and meanwhile, check that all of your shrimp is peeled and de-veined.
4) Add the shrimp into the slow cooker and cook for an additional 20 minutes, or until you can see that your shrimp are cooked through.

Serving Suggestion: If you're anything like me, you love your naan bread! Sometimes, when I'm counting the calories, I forego the rice and just enjoy a coriander naan bread with my curry to soak up all the sauce!

Tip: If you want to make your own red curry paste, try this; take 10 dried chillies and leave them to soak in warm water for 20 minutes, and then finely chop them. Then, add 1 teaspoon of cumin seeds, 2 teaspoons of coriander seeds and ½ a teaspoon of black peppercorns into a pan to toast and begin to become fragrant. Then, once they're cooled, grind them up into a powder, and mix them together with the chopped chillies, 1 stalk of chopped lemongrass (the white part only), 1 teaspoon of minced ginger, 6 finely chopped coriander roots, 2 finely chopped shallots, 4 chopped cloves of garlic, 2 teaspoons of shrimp paste or fish sauce, and an additional 8 chopped chillies. Blend the mixture with ¼ of a cup of water until smooth. The leftover paste can be frozen!

8. Fish Tacos

Serves: 6

Preparation time: 15 minutes + 2-1/2 hours cooking time

Ingredients:

- 18 oz canned tomatoes (if you can find one that includes chilli too, you'll get a nice kick!)
- 6 frozen fish fillets
- 2 tablespoons lime juice
- 1/4 cup fresh cilantro
- Soft taco shells

Direction:

1) Place the fish fillets into the bottom of the slow cooker.
2) Chop up the fresh cilantro, and add it into the cooker, along with the canned tomato, lime juice and a good pinch of salt and

pepper.
3) Cook on Low for 6 hours, until you can flake up the fish fillets with a fork.
4) Spoon the filling into the soft taco shells and enjoy!

Serving Suggestion: A chilli salad and guacamole make this a light and fresh dinner, perfect for summer!

Tip: A cheap fish that is perfect for this type of dish is tilapia. It flakes up super easily, so this really is a great way to use it!

9. Citrus Fish

Serves: 4

Preparation time: 15 minutes + 1-1/2 hours cooking time

Ingredients:

- ☐ 5 tablespoons fresh parsley
- ☐ 4 white fish fillets
- ☐ 1 onion
- ☐ 1 orange
- ☐ 1 lemon

Direction:

1) Rub salt and pepper into the fish fillets and place them into the slow cooker.
2) Zest the orange and lemon, chop up the parsley and peel and dice the onion. Mix them all together.
3) Sprinkle the zests, parsley and onion all over the fish fillets.
4) Slice up the orange and lemon and place the slices on top of the fish fillets.
5) Cook on Low for 90 minutes.

Serving Suggestion: A lightly herby couscous that won't overpower the delicate citrus flavours is the perfect accompaniment to this citrus fish.

Tip: Although you can get cheap white fish, this is often very crumbly and flaky. To serve this properly as fillets, try something that holds together more, like cod.

10. Haddock Chowder

Serves: 2

Preparation time: 15 minutes + 1 hour cooking time

Ingredients:

- ☐ 17 fl oz milk
- ☐ 12-1/4 oz potatoes
- ☐ 10-1/2 oz frozen haddock fillet
- ☐ 5 oz frozen sweet corn
- ☐ 1 tablespoon butter

Direction:

1) Peel and slice up the potatoes.
2) Add the potatoes into a saucepan with the milk. Season well with salt and pepper and bring it to the boil. Let it simmer for 5 minutes, and then tip everything into the slow cooker.
3) Add in the haddock fillets and sweet corn and cook on High for 1 hour.
4) Stir in the butter and serve.

Serving Suggestion: Can't beat crusty bread!

Tip: Haddock is a pretty strong flavoured fish, especially if you use smoked. If you're trying to make kids eat this dish, you may have more success to begin with using a less 'fishy' fish, like cod or tilapia.

11. Lemon Pepper Tilapia

Serves: 4

Preparation time: 15 minutes + 1 hour cooking time

Ingredients:

- ☐ 10 tablespoons lemon juice
- ☐ 6 tilapia fillets
- ☐ 3 tablespoons butter
- ☐ 1 bundle of asparagus

Direction:

1) Cut a piece of foil for each fillet, and divide the asparagus evenly between them.
2) Lay the fillet of fish on top of the asparagus, and drizzle on lemon juice and sprinkle on a good amount of pepper.
3) Wrap up the foil and cook on High for 2 hours.

Serving Suggestion: Keep this super healthy by serving with more steamed vegetables.

Tip: You can use frozen fish fillets, just add an extra hour on to the cooking time.

12. Paprika Seafood Stew

Serves: 2

Preparation time: 15 minutes + 3-1/2 hours cooking time

Ingredients:

- ☐ 14 oz white fish
- ☐ 14 oz canned tomatoes
- ☐ 7 oz roasted red bell pepper
- ☐ 3 teaspoons paprika
- ☐ 2 onions

Direction:

1) Peel and slice up the onions and bell pepper if not already done.
2) Add them into the slow cooker, along with the canned tomatoes and paprika and cook on High for 3 hours.
3) Then, flake in the white fish and cook for a further 30 minutes before serving.

Serving Suggestion: Add in other kinds of seafood too to bulk it up and add more flavour if you like. I also love to make little garlic croutons to sprinkle on top.

Tip: To roast your bell peppers, slice them in half and de-seed them, and place them flesh side down an a baking tray. Bake in an oven at 450F for 25 minutes until the skins are wrinkled.

13. Fish with Salsa

Serves: 4

Preparation time: 15 minutes + 2 hours cooking time

Ingredients:

- ☐ 16 oz white fish
- ☐ 15 oz canned tomatoes
- ☐ 3 garlic cloves
- ☐ 1 bell pepper
- ☐ 1 onion

Direction:

1) Add 1/4 of a cup of water along with the canned tomatoes to the bottom of the slow cooker. Season with salt and pepper.
2) Peel and dice the onions and de-seed and dice up the bell pepper. Also peel and mince the garlic.
3) Stir all the vegetables into the tomato.
4) Rub salt and pepper onto the fish and place the fillets on top of the tomato mixture.
5) Cook on Low for 2 hours.

Serving Suggestion: Some fresh, fluffy rice is all you'll need with this delicious salsa.

Tip: If you like, you can rub other kinds of seasoning onto the fish too.

14. Salmon Bake

Serves: 4

Preparation time: 15 minutes + 2 hours cooking time

Ingredients:

- [ ] 48 oz canned salmon
- [ ] 16 oz canned tomatoes
- [ ] 4 cups breadcrumbs
- [ ] 1 green bell pepper
- [ ] 1 cup parmesan cheese

Direction:

1) Mix the canned salmon, flaking it up as you go, with the canned tomatoes. Season well with salt and pepper.
2) De-seed and slice up the green bell pepper and stir it into the mixture too.
3) Add the mixture into the bottom of the slow cooker.
4) Mix together the breadcrumbs and crumbed parmesan, and sprinkle them evenly over the top.
5) Cook on Low for 5 hours.

Serving Suggestion: I love this with a creamy potato gratin.

Tip: If you want a crunchier topping, you can place the bake under the broiler for a few minutes to crisp up.

15. Fish with Onion Sauce

Serves: 4
Preparation time: 15 minutes + 30 minutes cooking time

Ingredients:

- ☐ 5 garlic cloves
- ☐ 4 white fish fillets
- ☐ 4 red onions
- ☐ 1 cup dry white wine
- ☐ 1/4 cup fresh parsley

Direction:

1) Peel and slice 2 of the onions, and add them into a pan with a cup of water to begin softening.
2) Separately, peel and slice up the other 2 and begin frying them until crispy.
3) Mince the garlic in with the crispy onions.
4) Add all of the onion mixtures into the bottom of the slow cooker, and pour in another cup of water and the white wine.
5) Season well with salt and pepper and place the fish fillets on top.
6) Tear the fresh parsley and sprinkle it all over the top.
7) Cook on High for 30 minutes.

Serving Suggestion: This is actually a great gourmet lunch. Serve with fresh crusty bread to mop up all of the delicious sauce!

Tip: Once the fish is done, transfer all of the sauce into a pan and reduce ti down until it thickens nicely.

16. Saucy Fish Pie

Serves: 4

Preparation time: 30 minutes + 2-1/2 hours cooking time

Ingredients:

- ☐ 14 oz frozen fish mixture
- ☐ 14 oz potatoes
- ☐ 10 fl oz milk
- ☐ 3-1/2 oz butter
- ☐ 1-3/4 oz plain flour

Direction:

1) Peel and boil the potatoes, and then mash them to your liking, using some of the milk and butter to make it smooth and creamy.
2) Whilst the potatoes are boiling, you can begin making the sauce. Add half of the butter into a pan along with the flour. After a minute, take it off of the heat and pour in cold milk, a little at a time, whisking as you go to create a smooth sauce. Season with salt and pepper.
3) Rinse the fish pie mixture and spread it out along the bottom of the slow cooker.
4) Stir the sauce all over the fish mixture.
5) Spread the mashed potato all over the top, and season again with salt and pepper.
6) Cook on Low for 2-1/2 hours.

Serving Suggestion: Steamed veggies on the side round this up into a nutritious and balanced dinner.

Tip: If you're like me and you have the need for cheese, then sprinkle some on top and broil it until melted just before serving.

17. Herby Fish Fillets

Serves: 4

Preparation time: 10 minutes + 2-1/2 hours cooking time

Ingredients:

- ☐ 4 white fish fillets
- ☐ 4 garlic cloves
- ☐ 1/4 cup fresh basil
- ☐ 1/4 cup fresh parsley

Direction:

1) Take a piece of foil for each fillet, big enough to wrap all the way around it, and place the fillets in the centre.
2) Rub salt and pepper into each fillet, and then mince a garlic clove onto each.
3) Tear the basil and parsley over each fillet.
4) Wrap the foil up tightly around, but avoid crushing the fish.
5) Cook on Low for 2-1/2 hours.

Serving Suggestion: There are so many things you could do with these! On top of a couscous salad is a great idea, for example.

Tip: This technique is so versatile! You can change up your seasonings for the fish however you like. Try spicy fish, or pesto.

18. Vietnamese Braised Catfish

Serves: 4

Preparation time: 10 minutes + 6 hours cooking time

Ingredients:

- [ ] 4 catfish steaks
- [ ] 2 red chillies
- [ ] 2 inches fresh ginger
- [ ] 1/2 cup coconut sugar
- [ ] 1/4 cup fish sauce

Direction:

1) De-seed and slice up the chillies, and peel and mince the garlic cloves.
2) Put the coconut sugar into a pan and stir it until it melts.
3) Once it's caramelised, stir in the fish sauce, chillies and garlic.
4) Pour the sauce into the slow cooker, and add in the catfish steaks.
5) Cover the slow cooker and cook on Low for 6 hours.

Serving Suggestion: Noodles with fresh coriander are the perfect base for your steaks!

Tip: If you can't get hold of catfish, then tuna steaks will work nicely too.

19. Ginger Squid

Serves: 4

Preparation time: 10 minutes + 2-1/2 hours cooking time

Ingredients:

- ☐ 17-1/2 oz squid rings
- ☐ 5 garlic cloves
- ☐ 3 inches fresh ginger
- ☐ 1/2 cup brown sugar
- ☐ 1/4 cup soy sauce

Direction:

1) Peel and mince the garlic and ginger, and stir them together with the brown sugar and soy sauce.
2) Pour the mixture into the slow cooker, and add in ½ a cup of water.
3) Season with salt and pepper to taste, and add in the squid.
4) Cook on Low for 8 hours.

Serving Suggestion: This is a great party appetizer!

Tip: If you like it hot, throw some chillies in there too!

20. Crab Legs

Serves: 4

Preparation time: 10 minutes + 1-1/2 hours cooking time

Ingredients:

- ☐ 8-12 bunches crab legs
- ☐ 8 garlic cloves
- ☐ 2 teaspoons dried dill

- ☐   1 cup butter

Direction:

1) Rinse the crab legs, and place them into the slow cooker in a dish.
2) Add in water until just below the dish.
3) Melt the butter, and mince the garlic into it. Stir in the dill too, and season with salt and pepper.
4) Pour the butter mixture all over the crab legs and cook on Low for 1-1/2 hours.

Serving Suggestion: Go for a Southern feast by serving with cheese grits!

Tip: Frozen crab legs may be cheaper than frozen, and work just as well! You may just need to give them an extra 30 minutes in the slow cooker.

21. Coconut Mussels

Serves: 4

Preparation time: 20 minutes + 2-1/4 hours cooking time

Ingredients:

- ☐   32 oz fresh mussels
- ☐   2 garlic cloves
- ☐   1-1/2 cups coconut milk
- ☐   1 chilli
- ☐   1/2 cup fresh cilantro

Direction:

1) Season one cup of water well with salt and pepper, and pour it into the bottom of the slow cooker.
2) Chop up the chilli and peel and mince the garlic, and add them into the slow cooker too.
3) Cook this mixture on High for 2 hours.
4) Meanwhile, check that all of the mussels are cleaned, scrubbed and de-bearded.
5) Then, add the mussels, fresh cilantro and coconut milk into the slow cooker and cook for another 15 minutes on High, until the mussels have opened.

Serving Suggestion: Serve with Asian greens and garlic bread for a delicious meal.

Tip: Remember to remove any mussels that do not open when being steamed, as this means they're bad.

Vegetarian / Vegan Dishes

1. Chickpea Stew

Serves: 6

Preparation time: 20 minutes + 3-1/4 hours cooking time

Ingredients:

- ☐ 3 carrots
- ☐ 2 potatoes
- ☐ 2 sprigs of thyme
- ☐ 1-1/2 onion

Direction:

1) Have the chickpeas soaking in water overnight before using.
2) Peel and chop the carrots, onion and potatoes.
3) Into the slow cooker, add the soaked chickpeas, chopped carrots, onion, thyme, 8 cups of water and a good seasoning of salt and pepper.
4) Cook on High for 90 minutes, before adding in the potatoes and cooking on Low for a further 1 hour and 45 minutes.

Serving Suggestion: For a hearty meal on a cold evening, why not serve with warm, fresh bread?

Tip: For more of a soup, you can take half of the mixture and puree it with a little water, and then mix it back in with the whole ingredients. The choice is yours!

2. Mac & Cheese

Serves: 6

Preparation time: 20 minutes + 4 hours cooking time

Ingredients:

- ☐ 16 oz elbow macaroni
- ☐ 16 oz shredded cheddar cheese
- ☐ 12 fl oz milk
- ☐ 4 eggs
- ☐ 1-1/2 cups cream

Direction:

1) Cook the macaroni until 'al dente' according to the package instructions.
2) Meanwhile, whisk together the milk, eggs, cream and 2/3 of the cheese, seasoning well with salt and pepper.
3) Stir the sauce through the cooked macaroni, and then pour the whole thing into your slow cooker.
4) Sprinkle the remaining cheese all over the top of the macaroni mixture and cook on High for 3 hours, before reducing it to Low to cook for a final hour.

Serving Suggestion: I feel that mac & cheese is an awesome meal on its own, but if you are worried about nutritional value, then serve with a fresh side salad.

Tip: Experiment with different types of cheeses, if you like. I often find in my local supermarket jalapeno cheddar, which adds a great kick to this dish!

3. Cauliflower Curry

Serves: 6

Preparation time: 10 minutes + 4 hours cooking time

Ingredients:

- 28 oz cauliflower florets
- 14 oz canned tomatoes
- 2 tablespoons ginger
- 1-1/2 tablespoons curry powder
- 1 onion

Direction:

1) Into the slow cooker, add the canned tomatoes. Stir in the curry powder and ginger and a dash of salt and pepper.
2) Peel and dice the onion and chop the cauliflower into small florets and add everything into the slow cooker too.
3) Cook on High for 4 hours until the cauliflower is nicely softened.

Serving Suggestion: What goes better with curry than rice and naan bread? Nothing!

Tip: As ever with this kind of dish, feel free to play with the level of spices to fit your taste.

4. Quinoa Stuffed Bell Peppers

Serves: 6

Preparation time: 10 minutes + 4 hours cooking time

Ingredients:

- [ ] 16 oz canned black beans
- [ ] 6 bell peppers
- [ ] 1-1/2 cups canned tomatoes
- [ ] 1-1/2 teaspoons chilli powder
- [ ] 1 cup quinoa

Direction:

1) Chop the tops off of the peppers, and carefully scrape out the seeds.
2) Blend the canned tomatoes into a sauce.

3) Drain the beans and mix them together with the quinoa, canned tomatoes and chilli powder. Season well with salt and pepper.
4) Divide the quinoa mixture evenly between the peppers.
5) Into the bottom of the slow cooker, pour ½ of a cup of water. Then, place the peppers in so that they're sitting in the water.
6) Cook on High for 3 hours.

Serving Suggestion: Jazz these up with all kinds of toppings! Create a 'topping bar' and let everyone load up on their own. Avocado, salsa, raw onions and fresh herbs are all great toppers!

Tip: These are great as a make ahead and refrigerate meal. You can refrigerate the leftovers and take them for an easy lunch the next day!

5. Garlic Hoisin Mushrooms

Serves: 6
Preparation time: 10 minutes + 3 hours cooking time

Ingredients:

- 24 of fresh button mushrooms
- 6 garlic cloves
- 1/2 cup hoisin sauce
- 1/2 teaspoon chilli flakes

Direction:

1) Mince the garlic and mix it together with the hoisin sauce, chilli

flakes and ¼ of a cup of water.
2) Peel the mushrooms and rinse them, and then add them into the slow cooker.
3) Pour the sauce all over the mushrooms and stir well to coat them and season with salt and pepper.
4) Cook on High for 3 hours.

Serving Suggestion: Serve the mushrooms on a bed of rice and steamed broccoli, with the cooking sauce drizzled over the top.

Tip: If you want to make your own hoisin sauce, you simply need to combine soy sauce, peanut butter, brown sugar, rice wine vinegar, garlic, sesame oil, chilli and black pepper to make the blend to your liking.

6. Eggplant Parmesan

Serves: 6
Preparation time: 10 minutes + 4 hours cooking time

Ingredients:

- 12 oz mozzarella
- 2 eggplants
- 2 eggs
- 2 cups tomato sauce
- 1 cup panko crumbs

Direction:

1) Slice the eggplants into ½ inch discs.
2) Sprinkle each slice with salt and pepper and lay them on a lined baking tray. Leave them to sit for 30 minutes and then pat them dry.
3) Pour 1/3 of the tomato sauce into the bottom of the slow cooker.
4) Season the breadcrumbs with salt and pepper.
5) Whisk the eggs, and dip each piece of eggplant into the egg, before dipping it into the breadcrumb mixture to coat it on both sides.
6) Add a layer of eggplant slices into the slow cooker, and then pour in some more tomato sauce.
7) Continue the eggplant and tomato sauce layers until you run out, and then layer the mozzarella on top.
8) Cook on High for 4 hours.

Serving Suggestion: Alongside a big green salad makes a

great lunch or dinner.

Tip: This recipe is pretty basic, but you can add in spices and herbs to your taste.

7. Vegetable Omelette

Serves: 6

Preparation time: 10 minutes + 4 hours cooking time

Ingredients:

- ☐ 6 eggs
- ☐ 1 onion
- ☐ 1 red bell pepper
- ☐ 1 cup broccoli florets
- ☐ 1/2 cup milk

Direction:

1) Lightly grease the bottom of the slow cooker.
2) Whisk together the eggs and milk with a good pinch of salt and pepper.
3) Peel and dice the onion, and de-seed and slice up the bell pepper.
4) Add all of the vegetables into the bottom of the slow cooker, and then pour the egg mixture all over the top.
5) Cook on High for 1 hour and 45 minutes.

Serving Suggestion: If this is going to be more of a dinner that's being served rather than a snack for one, garnish it to look pretty with halved cherry tomatoes and fresh herbs on top.

Tip: Can you really ever have enough vegetables? The answer is no! Chuck in whatever else you have to enjoy even more goodness in this omelette!

8. Spaghetti Squash Thai Noodles

Serves: 2

Preparation time: 15 minutes + 6 hours cooking time

Ingredients:

- 6 tablespoons Thai sauce (recipe found in tips)
- 2 cups broccoli
- 1 spaghetti squash
- 1 tablespoon sesame seeds
- 1 tablespoon chopped peanuts

Direction:

1) Pierce the spaghetti squash all over with a fork, and place it into the slow cooker.
2) Pour in 2 cups of water and cook on Low for 6 hours.
3) Then, add in the broccoli florets, and continue to cook for another 2 hours.
4) When the squash has turned brown, allow it to cool until you can handles it, then cut it in half and scrape out the seeds and pulp and discard them.
5) Use a fork to shred the inside of the squash so that you get

your 'spaghetti'.
6) Season the 'spaghetti' with salt and pepper, and toss it together with the broccoli, sesame seeds and peanuts.

Serving Suggestion: Since this is low calorie, and you can only really get 2 servings from one spaghetti squash, why not enjoy this for dinner one day, and have the leftovers for a healthy lunch at work the next day?

Tip: To make your own Thai sauce, and have leftovers for next time, follow these instructions! Mix together 3 tablespoons of brown sugar, 6 tablespoons of peanut oil, 6 tablespoons of rice wine vinegar, 2 tablespoons of soy sauce, 2 tablespoons of grated ginger root, 4 minced garlic cloves, 2 teaspoons of sesame oil, 1 teaspoon of sriracha, a pinch of salt and some sesame seeds.

9. Mushroom Stroganoff

Serves: 2

Preparation time: 15 minutes + 6 hours cooking time

Ingredients:

- 22 oz button mushrooms
- 3 garlic cloves
- 2 teaspoons smoked paprika
- 1 cup vegetable stock
- 1 tablespoon sour cream

Direction:

1) Clean and peel the mushrooms, and chop up any larger ones into halves or quarters.
2) Add the mushrooms into the slow cooker, and mince in the garlic too.
3) Pour in the vegetable stock and stir in the smoked paprika. Also, season with salt and pepper to taste.
4) Then, leave it to cook on High for 4 hours.
5) Then, before serving, stir in the sour cream and season again to taste if necessary.

Serving Suggestion: Serve with brown rice and sprinkled with fresh parsley.

Tip: To bulk this out more, you can add in other vegetables too, such as onions and green bell peppers.

10. 'Baked' Potatoes

Serves: 4

Preparation time: 15 minutes + 8 hours cooking time

Ingredients:

☐ 4 baking potatoes

Direction:

1) Scrub your potatoes clean.
2) Dry them and pierce holes all over them, before wrapping them in aluminium foil.
3) Cook on Low for 8 hours.

Serving Suggestion: Well, how to top your baked potatoes is a very personal business! I would team them up with the cowboy beans found in this book, but what you decide is up to you!

Tip: To make this dish 'quicker' (although still not particularly quick, obviously!), you can cook on High for 4 hours.

11. Hash Brown Casserole

Serves: 6

Preparation time: 25 minutes + 5 hours cooking time

Ingredients:

- ☐ 32 oz potatoes
- ☐ 11 fl oz cream of mushroom soup
- ☐ 3 garlic cloves
- ☐ 3 cups shredded cheese
- ☐ 1 onion

Direction:

1) Peel your potatoes and grate them.
2) Peel and dice the onion and begin softening it in a pan. Peel and mince the garlic in too.
3) Put the potatoes into the slow cooker and pour in the onion and garlic, cream of mushroom soup and cheese and stir everything together until well mixed.
4) Cook on Low for 5 hours.

Serving Suggestion: Serve as part of an exciting Sunday brunch! (Although, of course, they'll be no sleeping in for you, as you'll have to be up at the crack of dawn to have these cooking for 5 hours and be ready in time!)

Tip: I like to fold in jalapenos sometimes too for a bit of a fun kick.

12. Spinach & Ricotta Lasagne

Serves: 6

Preparation time: 20 minutes + 3 hours cooking time

Ingredients:

- ☐ 32 oz canned tomatoes
- ☐ 24 oz ricotta cheese
- ☐ 9 lasagne sheets
- ☐ 4 cups spinach
- ☐ 2 cups mozzarella

Direction:

1) Season the canned tomatoes with salt and pepper, and blend half up them up until smooth. Then, mix the blended part back together with the other half.
2) Spread 1/2 of a cup of the tomatoes along the bottom of the slow cooker.
3) Cover the bottom of the slow cooker with some of the lasagne sheets.
4) Then, add on a layer of ricotta, a layer of spinach, a layer of tomato sauce, a layer of mozzarella and another layer of lasagne

sheets. Repeat until you've used up all of your ingredients.
5) Cook on High for 3 hours.

Serving Suggestion: For me there are 2 unquestionable sides for lasagne... garlic bread and sweet potato wedges.

Tip: Cook for up to another 2 hours for a more solid and less saucy lasagne. Depends how you like it!

13. Veggie Vindaloo

Serves: 6

Preparation time: 15 minutes + 3 hours cooking time

Ingredients:

- 6 oz tomato paste
- 4 carrots
- 4 cups cauliflower florets
- 2 zucchini
- 1/2 cup vindaloo paste (recipe in tips)

Direction:

1) Peel and chop the carrots and chop up the zucchini. Mix them together with the cauliflower florets and place them into the slow cooker.
2) Mix together the tomato paste and vindaloo paste with ¼ of a cup of water, and pour the sauce all over the veggies.
3) Cook on Low for 3 hours.

Serving Suggestion: It's all about the garlic & coriander naan, baby!

Tip: If you want to make your own vindaloo paste, here's how; blend together 3 garlic cloves, 2 inches of fresh ginger, 1 date, 1-1/2 teaspoons of ground coriander seeds, 1-1/4 teaspoons of cumin, 1/2 a teaspoon of mustard powder, 1/2 a teaspoon of cayenne, 1/2 a teaspoon of turmeric and 1/4 of a teaspoon of cardamom with 1/2 a cup of water. Any leftovers can be stored in the refrigerator for 3-4 days.

14. Saag Aloo

Serves: 4

Preparation time: 20 minutes + 2-1/2 hours cooking time

Ingredients:

- 24 oz potatoes
- 10 oz spinach
- 1 onion
- 1 teaspoon cumin
- 1 teaspoon ground coriander

Direction:

1) Peel and chop up the potatoes, and add them into the slow cooker with 1 ½ fl oz of water.
2) Peel and slice up the onion, and add it in too.
3) Sprinkle in the cumin and coriander, and season well with salt and pepper.

4) Top with the spinach and cook on High for 2-1/2 hours.

Serving Suggestion: For me, this is very much the exciting side dish when it comes to Indian food! I often forego the rice entirely and have a side of saag aloo with my curry. Or, if you're just looking for a small meal, have this with a side of naan bread.

Tip: The sky is the limit when it comes to spices! Taste after about an hour, and add in more if you feel that you need more flavour!

15. Cheese & Tomato Pasta

Serves: 4

Preparation time: 10 minutes + 2-1/2 hours cooking time

Ingredients:

- ☐ 56 oz canned tomatoes
- ☐ 16 oz penne pasta
- ☐ 2 teaspoons dried basil
- ☐ 1-3/4 cups mozzarella
- ☐ 1 onion

Direction:

1) Mix the dried basil and a good pinch of salt and pepper into the canned tomatoes and pour them into the slow cooker.
2) Peel and dice the onion and stir it in too.
3) Cook on Low for 2 hours.
4) Meanwhile, cook the penne according the package directions, and then stir it through the tomato sauce.

5) Shred the mozzarella on top of the dish and cook for a further 20 minutes.

Serving Suggestion: It has to be garlic bread, doesn't it?

Tip: Use a mixture of different cheeses if you like, for a little more range of flavour.

16. Mushroom Risotto

Serves: 4

Preparation time: 20 minutes + 1 hour cooking time

Ingredients:

- ☐ 27 fl oz vegetable stock
- ☐ 8-3/4 oz mushrooms
- ☐ 7 oz wholegrain rice
- ☐ 1-3/4 oz porcini mushrooms
- ☐ 1 onion

Direction:

1) Peel and slice up the onion and begin softening it a pan.
2) Peel and slice up the mushrooms too, and add them into the pan along with the onion.
3) Boil a little of the stock, and add the porcini into it to soak for 5 minutes.
4) Add the onions and mushrooms into the slow cooker, along with the rice, and pour in the remaining stock.
5) Finally, pour in the stock and porcini and cook on High for 1 hour.

Serving Suggestion: A glass of white wine and a sprinkling of fresh parsley on top finish this off a treat!

Tip: Risotto is notoriously hard to get right. This recipe has been tried and tested, and the main thing we can advise is do NOT open the lid before the hour is up!

17. Sweet Potato & Coconut Curry

Serves: 6

Preparation time: 20 minutes + 7 hours cooking time

Ingredients:

- [ ] 35 oz sweet potatoes
- [ ] 14 fl oz coconut milk
- [ ] 3 garlic cloves
- [ ] 2 red chillies
- [ ] 2 tablespoons peanut butter

Direction:

1) Mince the garlic into a pan and begin softening it for just a minute or 2.
2) De-seed and slice up the chillies, and add them into the pan too, until they become fragrant.
3) Peel and dice up the sweet potatoes, and add them into the pan just for 5 minutes to begin browning. Stir them around well.
4) Add the potato mixture into the slow cooker, and pour the coconut milk in too.
5) Top up with 8-10 fl oz of water, seasoned well with salt and pepper.
6) Cook on High for 7 hours.

Serving Suggestion: You can use this as a sauce and add in other veggies to bulk out the curry, or have it as the curry by itself and serve with rice.

Tip: If you want a chunkier curry sauce, you can replace the water content with canned tomatoes.

18. Butternut Squash & Cider Stew

Serves: 6

Preparation time: 15 minutes + 5 hours cooking time

Ingredients:

- 24 oz peeled butternut squash
- 2 garlic cloves
- 1-1/2 cups apple cider
- 1 cup canned tomatoes
- 1 teaspoon garam masala

Direction:

1) Dice up the squash and add it into a pan with a little water, salt and pepper to begin browning.
2) Mince in the garlic and sprinkle on the garam masala and stir everything around together.
3) Add everything into the slow cooker, and pour in the cider and tomatoes.
4) Cover and cook on Low for 4 hours.

Serving Suggestion: For a low calorie lunch, enjoy a bowl of this with a dollop of plain yoghurt on top, and a sprinkling of seeds.

Tip: If you have other similar vegetables, like turnips, parsnips and pumpkin then you can use them as well as the squash.

19. Arrabiata

Serves: 8

Preparation time: 10 minutes + 4 hours cooking time

Ingredients:

- ☐ 32 oz canned tomatoes
- ☐ 4 garlic cloves
- ☐ 1 onion
- ☐ 1 tablespoon chilli flakes
- ☐ 1/4 cup red wine

Direction:

1) Peel and dice up the garlic and onion and begin softening them in a pan.
2) Then, add them into the slow cooker, along with the wine, canned tomatoes and chilli flakes. Season w ell with salt and pepper.
3) Cook on Low for 4 hours.

Serving Suggestion: Enjoy as a spicy spread on ciabatta bread, or with pasta.

Tip: This sauce is famously very spicy, so feel free to add in more or less chilli to your taste.

20. Tomato & Basil Couscous

Serves: 6

Preparation time: 10 minutes + 15 minutes cooking time

Ingredients:

- ☐ 28 oz canned tomatoes
- ☐ 2-1/2 cups couscous
- ☐ 4 garlic cloves
- ☐ 2 onions
- ☐ 1/2 cup fresh basil

Direction:

1) Peel and dice the onion and garlic and begin softening them in a pan. Season them well with salt and pepper.
2) Boil 2-1/2 cups of water, and season well.
3) Place the water into the slow cooker, and add in the couscous.
4) Cook on Low for 10 minutes, and then stir in the canned tomatoes, onion and garlic.
5) Leave it for a further 5 minutes, and then tear the fresh basil on top to serve.

Serving Suggestion: Perfect to take in a handy pot wherever you go! Take it to work for lunch and be the envy of the whole office!

Tip: Add in some chilli flakes for an extra kick if you like!

21. Cornbread

Serves: 6
Preparation time: 10 minutes + 2 hours cooking time

Ingredients:

- ☐ 2 eggs
- ☐ 2 cups buttermilk
- ☐ 1-1/2 cups cornmeal
- ☐ 1-1/2 cups plain flour
- ☐ 1 tablespoon baking powder

Direction:

1) Stir together the cornmeal, plain flour and baking powder. Add in a pinch of salt.
2) Stir together the eggs and buttermilk, and stir them through the cornmeal mixture, until everything is nicely incorporated.
3) Melt the butter, and spread it around the bottom of the slow cooker.
4) Then, pour in the cornbread batter and spread it out evenly.
5) Cook on High for 2 hours.

Serving Suggestion: Spread on PB&J for a delightful afternoon snack!

Tip: Use yellow cornmeal for a more pleasing colour.

22. Spinach & Broccoli

Pudding

Serves: 6

Preparation time: 15 minutes + 4 hours cooking time

Ingredients:

- 16 oz baguette
- 12 eggs
- 10 oz baby leaf spinach
- 10 oz broccoli florets
- 2 cups milk

Direction:

1) Wilt the spinach by pouring boiling water over it, and then drain it and chop it up.
2) Chop the baguette up into cubes, and layer half of it into the bottom of a greased slow cooker.
3) Layer on the chopped spinach and broccoli.
4) Top with the remaining bread cubes.
5) Whisk together the milk and eggs, and season well with salt and pepper.
6) Pour the mixture all over the pudding and cook on Low for 3 1/2 hours.

Serving Suggestion: Add on some shredded cheese and stick the pudding under the grill before serving.

Tip: This is great for breakfast, but will also keep refrigerated for a few days and does good in the microwave when you have leftovers!

Appetizers

1. Spinach, Artichoke & Blue Cheese Dip

Serves: 24

Preparation time: 20 minutes + 3 hours cooking time

Ingredients:

28 oz canned artichoke hearts
12 oz creamy blue cheese
10 oz spinach
3 garlic cloves
1 cup light mayonnaise

Direction:

Into the slow cooker, add the artichoke hearts, spinach, mayonnaise and blue cheese.
Mince the garlic and add it in too, and stir everything well together. Cook on Low for 3 minutes.

Serving Suggestion: Serve as an appetizer at a party with seedy crackers for dipping.

Tip: If 100% blue cheese in this will be a bit much for you, try a 50/50 mix of blue cheese and mild cream cheese.

2. Lemon & Herb Snack Mix

Serves: 24

Preparation time: 10 minutes + 1-1/4 hours cooking time

Ingredients:

- ☐ 8 cups nut, seed & cracker mix of your choice
- ☐ 2 tablespoons dried dill
- ☐ 2 tablespoons olive oil
- ☐ 1 tablespoons lemon peel
- ☐ 1 teaspoon dried rosemary

Direction:

1) Toss the dill and rosemary through the nut, seed & cracker mix and add it into the slow cooker.
2) Drizzle the olive oil over the top and mix around to coat everything well.
3) Cook on High for 1 hour.
4) Then, sprinkle in the lemon peel and stir it around. Cook for another 15 minutes.

Serving Suggestion: These are perfect to serve in bowls as a pre-dinner snack at a gathering.

Tip: To make it easier to get your snack mix out, line the slow cooker with aluminium foil first and then just lift it out.

3. Bourbon Glazed Cocktail Sausages

Serves: 10

Preparation time: 10 minutes + 4 hours cooking time

Ingredients:

- [ ] 16 oz cooked mini cocktail sausages
- [ ] 3 tablespoons maple syrup
- [ ] 2 tablespoons Bourbon
- [ ] 1 teaspoon tapioca
- [ ] 1/3 cup apricot preserve

Direction:

1) Mix together the maple syrup, Bourbon, tapioca and apricot preserve.
2) Place the cocktail sausages into the slow cooker and then pour the sauce all over them.
3) Cook on Low for 4 hours.

Serving Suggestion: Skewer each sausage on a little cocktail stick, and serve with the sauce on the side for dipping.

Tip: Make a kid-friendly version by simply replacing the Bourbon with orange juice or plain old water!

4. Jalapeno Poppers

Makes: 10

Preparation time: 20 minutes + 3 hours cooking time

Ingredients:

- [ ] 10 jalapenos
- [ ] 8 slices bacon

- ☐ 4 oz cream cheese
- ☐ 1/3 cup grated parmesan
- ☐ 1/4 cup sour cream

Direction:

1) Chop off the tops of the jalapenos, and scrape out the seeds.
2) Fry the bacon until crispy and crumble it up.
3) Stir the bacon together with the cream cheese, sour cream and parmesan.
4) Fill the jalapenos with the stuffing mixture.
5) Pour 1/3 of a cup of water into the bottom of the slow cooker, and lay the jalapenos inside..
6) Cook on High for 3 hours, until the skin of the jalapenos looks wrinkly.

Serving Suggestion: If you think your diners may be a little wimpy, make a cooling ranch dipping sauce to help cool them down!

Tip: Maybe use gloves when chopping up the jalapenos... if you forget and touch your eyes later, you'll be in a world of pain!

5. Fondue

Serves: 10

Preparation time: 5 minutes + 2 hours cooking time

Ingredients:

- ☐ 16 oz Swiss cheese
- ☐ 16 oz cheddar

- [ ] 12 fl oz beer
- [ ] 11 fl oz cream of cheddar soup
- [ ] 1/2 teaspoon hot sauce

Direction:

1) Chop the cheddar and Swiss cheese up into cubes and place them into the slow cooker.
2) Pour in the beer and soup, as well as the hot sauce.
3) Cook on Low for 1 hour, before serving and seasoning with salt and pepper to taste.
4) Cook for another hour and then whisk until smooth before serving.

Serving Suggestion: Who can tell you what to dip in your fondue?? Try bread cubes, crackers or raw veggies.

Tip: Adjust the levels of hot sauce to your taste!

6. Guinness Cheese Dip

Serves: 16
Preparation time: 30 minutes

Ingredients:

- [ ] 32 oz cheddar or red Leicester cheese
- [ ] 2 tablespoons Worcestershire sauce
- [ ] 1 cup Guinness
- [ ] 1 teaspoon chilli powder
- [ ] 1/2 cup tomato salsa

Direction:

1) Chop the cheese up into cubes and add it into the slow cooker. Cover and cook on Low for 20 minutes until the cheese melts.
2) Then, add in the Guinness, Worcestershire sauce, tomato salsa and chilli powder and leave it cooking for a further 10 minutes.
3) Give it a good stir and pour into your serving dish.

Serving Suggestion: Top with chopped green onions and serve with nachos for a great snack whilst your guests wait for the main course!

Tip: You will want to serve this dip pretty quickly, as the cheese can begin to harden again, but become a strange texture which may not be quite so delicious!

7. Teriyaki Chicken Wings

Makes: 24

Preparation time: 2 hours marinating time + 4 hours cooking time

Ingredients:

- ☐ 24 chicken wings
- ☐ 1 cup soy sauce
- ☐ 1 teaspoon garlic powder
- ☐ 1/2 cup brown sugar
- ☐ 1/4 cup pineapple juice

Direction:

1) Mix together the soy sauce, garlic powder, brown sugar and pineapple juice. Pour the mixture all over the chicken wings and set aside for at least 2 hours to marinate.
2) Place the chicken wings into the slow cooker, along with 1 cup of the marinade.
3) Cook on High for 4 hours and enjoy!

Serving Suggestion: Sprinkle with chopped green onion and delight your diners with a blue cheese ranch dipping sauce.

Tip: If you are not a chicken wing fan (first of all, things kind of weird!), you can use chicken drumsticks too.

8. Bourbon Cowboy Baked Beans

Serves: 8

Preparation time: 25 minutes + 12 hours cooking time + 2 hours sitting

Ingredients:

- ☐ 16 oz dry white beans
- ☐ 10 slices thick cut bacon
- ☐ 1 onion
- ☐ 1 cup Bourbon
- ☐ 1 cup barbecue sauce

Direction:

1) The night beforehand, leave the beans soaking. Drain them the next day.

2) Put the beans into a large pan and set them to boil. Let them simmer for 40 minutes.
3) Meanwhile, cook the bacon until crispy and then remove from the pan.
4) Keeping the bacon fat in the pan, peel and dice the onion and fry it in there.
5) Mix together the barbecue sauce and the Bourbon.
6) Add the beans into the slow cooker, along with the onion and the fat from the pan, and the barbecue sauce mixture.
7) Chop up the bacon and add it in too.
8) Cook on Low for 12 hours, and then let the beans sit in the cooker after turning it off for at least another 2 hours, if not overnight.

Serving Suggestion: Serve with nachos for dipping in as a 'tide you over' dish before the main meal is ready!

Tip: Do not skip the 'sitting' part. This is where the sauce will begin to become thick and not liquid-y, just like how we want our beans!

9. Red Onion Chutney

Serves: 16+

Preparation time: 25 minutes + 12 hours cooking time + 2 hours sitting

Ingredients:

- ☐ 8 red onions
- ☐ 3-1/2oz caster sugar

- ☐ 3-1/2 fl oz red wine
- ☐ 3 fl oz red wine vinegar
- ☐ 2 star anise

Direction:

Peel and slice up the onions.
Place them into the slow cooker, and stir in the caster sugar, red wine and red wine vinegar.
Place in your star anise and cook on Low for 6 hours.
Remember to remove the star anise before serving.

Serving Suggestion:
Make a delightful little entree with a slice of crusty French bread, goats' cheese and a dollop of onion chutney.

Tip:
Do take care with how you slice your onions. Do not dice them. Try to aim for thin slices.

10. Sweet & Spicy Nuts

Serves: 8+

Preparation time: 5 minutes + 1 hours cooking time + 1 hour sitting

Ingredients:

- ☐ 4 cups mixed nuts of your choice
- ☐ 1 teaspoon ground ginger
- ☐ 1/2 cup brown sugar
- ☐ 1/3 cup butter

☐ 1/4 teaspoon cayenne pepper

Direction:

1) Ensure that all of your nuts have their skins or shells removed and add them all into the slow cooker.
2) Melt the butter, and mix into it the brown sugar, ginger and cayenne.
3) Pour the butter mixture all over the nuts, and stir to coat them well.
4) Cook on Low for 1 hour. Then, spread the nuts out in a single layer on a baking tray lined with foil to crisp up a little more for about an hour.

Serving Suggestion: Having a dinner party? Have a few bowls of these dotted around for your guests to dip into as they mingle.

Tip: Some nuts are really best roasted first, such as almonds, hazelnuts and pecans.

Side Dishes

1. Red Beans

Serves: 6

Preparation time: 20 minutes + 3-1/4 hours cooking time

Ingredients:

- 16 oz red kidney beans
- 8 oz cured sausage
- 3 garlic cloves
- 1 onion
- 1 tablespoon Creole seasoning (recipe in Tip)

Direction:

1) Place the beans into your slow cooker and cover with boiling water up to 2 inches above the beans. Cover the pot and leave them soaking for an hour.
2) Meanwhile, peel and dice the onion and garlic and brown them for a few minutes in a pan.
3) Slice up the sausage.
4) Drain the beans, and keep them in the slow cooker. Add in the garlic and onion, sausage, seasoning and 7 cups of water.
5) Cook on High for 90 minutes until the beans are tender.

Serving Suggestion: These are a great side to accompany nachos or tacos.

Tip: For Creole seasoning, you can process together into a powder paprika, garlic powder, black pepper, onion powder, cayenne pepper, dried oregano and dried thyme. Adjust the quantities to your taste.

2. Cheese Grits

Serves: 8

Preparation time: 10 minutes + 8 hours soaking time + 2 hours cooking time

Ingredients:

- 2 cups uncooked grits
- 2 tablespoons butter
- 1 cup shredded cheddar cheese
- 1/2 cup parmesan cheese
- 1/4 cup cream

Direction:

1) Place the uncooked grits into the slow cooker and add in 6 cups of water. Let the grits settle for a minute or 2, and then skim any solids off of the top as these are the bad bits.
2) Cover the cooker and leave the grits soaking for 8 hours.
3) Then, cook on High for 1 hour, before stirring in the butter, cheddar cheese, parmesan cheese and cream, and season well with salt and pepper.
4) Cover and continue cooking on High for another hour.

Serving Suggestion: Simply pan fry some shrimp and serve on a bed of grits with fresh green onions for a super Southern dinner.

Tip: There will be nothing terrible in the grits, but there may still be some husks remaining, so we do recommend skimming a few times to be sure you're rid of it all.

3. Orange Sweet Potatoes

Serves: 8

Preparation time: 20 minutes + 4 hours cooking time

Ingredients:

- 64 oz sweet potatoes
- 4 tablespoons melted butter
- 3 tablespoons brown sugar
- 2 garlic cloves
- 1/2 cup no added sugar orange juice

Direction:

1) Peel the sweet potatoes (or simply scrub the skin), and shop them up into 1/4 inch thick rounds. Place them into the slow cooker.
2) Peel and mince the garlic and mix it together with the butter, orange juice and brown sugar.
3) Pour the mixture all over the sweet potatoes and cook on Low for 5-1/2 hours.

Serving Suggestion: Crumble crispy bacon in with these potatoes for a delicious salty kick. Dress with fresh parsley.

Tip: Having slender sweet potatoes works a little better when a recipe calls for rounds. It ensures that the slices are more likely to be even and therefore cook evenly.

4. Creamed Corn

Serves: 6

Preparation time: 10 minutes + 3-1/4 hours cooking time

Ingredients:

- 45 oz canned corn
- 8 oz cream cheese
- 1 cup milk
- 1 tablespoon sugar
- 1/2 cup firm butter

Direction:

1) Drain the corn and put it into the slow cooker.
2) Mix together the milk and sugar, along with a good pinch of salt and pepper, and pour this mixture all over the corn.
3) Chop the cream cheese and butter up into cubes and place them on top of the corn. Do not mix them in.
4) Cook for 3 hours on High heat. Then, stir everything together and cook for a further 15 minutes before serving.

Serving Suggestion: This is the perfect side for so many things! I personally love it with barbecue shredded chicken and salad. Light and delicious!

Tip: If you know you can handle a more pungent cheese, then feel free to switch some if not all of the cream cheese out for something stronger. Just keep it creamy still for the best results.

5. Asian Style Roasted Vegetables

Serves: 6

Preparation time: 10 minutes + 3-1/4 hours cooking time

Ingredients:

- 45 oz butternut squash
- 35 oz sweet potatoes
- 27 fl oz coconut milk
- 3 tablespoons soy sauce
- 2 tablespoons chilli paste

Direction:

1) Peel and chop up the butternut squash and sweet potatoes. Try to have fairly even chunks of about 2 inches. Place them into the slow cooker.
2) Whisk together the coconut milk, chilli paste and soy sauce with 12-1/2 fl oz of water. Season with salt, if necessary.
3) Pour the soy sauce mixture all over the vegetables.
4) Cook on High for 4 hours until the vegetables are tender.

Serving Suggestion: These would be the perfect side dish to an Asian-style roast. I'm thinking coconut braised beef, and other sides of bok choy and chilli-fried onions.

Tip: If you have other roasting vegetables, then go ahead and throw them in too!

Desserts

1. Almond Cheesecake

Serves: 6

Preparation time: 30 minutes + 3 hours cooking time

Ingredients:

- 15 oz cream cheese
- 3 teaspoons almond extract
- 2-1/2 tablespoons butter
- 2 eggs
- 3/4 cup cookie crumbs

Direction:

1) Melt the butter and mix it together with the cookie crumbs.
2) Then, press the crumb mixture down firmly and evenly into a cake tin that will fit inside your slow cooker.
3) Beat the cream cheese for 2 or 3 minutes, until smooth, and then beat in the eggs and stir in the almond extract, to taste.
4) Spread the cream cheese topping evenly over the crumb base.
5) Into the slow cooker, add water up to around ½ an inch depth. Then, fit in a rack and place the cake tin on top of it.
6) Drape a clean dish cloth over the cheesecake, and then fit the lid of the pot. Cook on High for 2 hours, before turning off the heat and letting it stand for another hour.
7) Refrigerate the cheesecake before serving.

Serving Suggestion: Some toasted almonds and a dollop of sweetened sour cream on the side would make this a delicious dessert.

Tip: If this will be a cheesecake for adults, replace some or all of the almond extract with almond liqueur!

2. Brownie Cake

Serves: 6

Preparation time: 10 minutes + 3 hours cooking time

Ingredients:

- ☐ 6 oz butter
- ☐ 3 eggs
- ☐ 1-1/2 cups sugar
- ☐ 2/3 cup cocoa powder
- ☐ 1/3 cup plain flour

Direction:

1) Line the bottom of the slow cooker with aluminium foil and grease it.
2) Melt the butter and whisk it together with the eggs, sugar, flour and cocoa powder.
3) Pour the batter evenly into the bottom of the slow cooker, smoothing it with a spatula.
4) Cook on Low for 3 hours. The cake should still be nice and gooey in the centre.

Serving Suggestion: Warm with a dollop of good vanilla ice cream is the way!

Tip: For extra chewy, gooiness, add in 2/3 of a cup of caramel pieces!

3. Cranberry Stuffed Apples

Serves: 4

Preparation time: 10 minutes + 4-1/2 hours cooking time

Ingredients:

- 4 medium apples
- 2 tablespoons walnuts
- 1/2 teaspoons cinnamon
- 1/3 cup cranberries
- 1/4 cup brown sugar

Direction:

1) Core the apples, but be sure to leave the bottom in tact or they'll just leak!
2) Peel the top third of each apple.
3) Chop up the walnuts and mix them together with the cranberries, brown sugar and cinnamon, and spoon the mixture into the apples.
4) Place them into the slow cooker.
5) Cook on Low for 4-1/2 hours.

Serving Suggestion: Whipped cream or ice cream, of

course!

Tip: If cranberries and walnuts aren't your thing, try other berries and nuts, such as blueberries and pecans.

4. Chocolate Fudge

Makes: 20 squares
Preparation time: 5 minutes + 1 hour cooking time

Ingredients:

- ☐ 2 cups milk chocolate chips
- ☐ 1 teaspoons vanilla extract
- ☐ 1/2 cup white chocolate chips
- ☐ 1/3 cup honey
- ☐ 1/4 cup heavy cream

Direction:

1) Pour the heavy cream into the slow cooker, and stir into it the milk chocolate chips and honey.
2) Cook on High for 1 hour.
3) Then, stir in the white chocolate chips and vanilla extract and leave cooking for another 10 minutes.
4) Pour the mixture into a lines baking tray and leave it to cool completely before cutting into small pieces.

Serving Suggestion: Sprinkle coarse sea salt on top for that incredible sweet and salty flavour mix.

Tip: If you want other flavours in your fudge, use other extracts than vanilla. Orange works really nicely, or a dash of peppermint.

5. Dulce De Leche

Makes: 3 jars

Preparation time: 5 minute + 10 hours cooking time

Ingredients:

- 28 oz sweetened condensed milk

Direction:

1) Rinse your jars well, and divide the sweetened condensed milk evenly between them.
2) Seal the jars with their rings and lids (ensure that they are well cleaned too!) Seal them tightly!
3) Place the jars into the slow cooker, ensuring that they are not touching.
4) Fill the slow cooker with water so that it comes up to an inch or 2 above the tops of the jars.
5) Cook on Low for 10 hours.

Serving Suggestion: The possibilities are endless with dulce de leche! Spread it on toast, bake it into your brownies, or drizzle it over a hot cup of cocoa topped with whipped cream – the sky is the limit!

Tip: Be SUPER careful when taking the jars out of the slow cooker because they will be unbelievably hot.

Soups, Broths & Stocks

1. Tortilla Soup

Serves: 6
Preparation time: 20 minutes + 4 hours cooking time

Ingredients:

- [ ] 15 oz canned tomatoes
- [ ] 4 onions
- [ ] 4 oz tortilla chips
- [ ] 3 teaspoons chilli powder
- [ ] 2 garlic cloves

Direction:

1) Peel and mince the garlic, and peel and slice the onions. Place them in a pan to begin softening.
2) Stir the chilli powder into the mix.
3) Add everything into the slow cooker, and tip in the canned tomatoes and 32 fl oz of well salted water.
4) Season the mixture with salt and pepper and cook on Low for 4 hours.
5) To serve, layer tortilla chips into the bottom of the bowls and ladle the soup on top. Add another layer of tortilla chips on top and enjoy!

Serving Suggestion: It makes sense to top with sour cream, avocado, green onions and shredded cheese too, does it not?

Tip: Make this meal go further by bulking the soup up with vegetables!

2. Sweet Potato & Peanut Soup

Serves: 6

Preparation time: 20 minutes + 4 hours cooking time

Ingredients:

- ☐ 40 oz sweet potatoes
- ☐ 15 oz canned tomatoes
- ☐ 2 inches fresh ginger
- ☐ 1 onion
- ☐ 1/4 cup creamy natural peanut butter

Direction:

1) Peel and dice the sweet potatoes and place them into the slow cooker.
2) Peel and dice the onion and ginger and add it to the cooker too. Season well with salt and pepper.
3) Add in the canned tomatoes and cook on High for 3 hours.
4) Stir in the peanut butter and leave it cooking for another hour.
5) Blend until smooth and season again with salt and pepper to taste.

Serving Suggestion: Smokey Pita Chips make a great side to dip into this soup. To make some, simply mince garlic into olive oil and smoked paprika. Slice pita bread into lengths or chips and brush the mixture all over them. Bake for 10 minutes until crispy and enjoy!

Tip: If you have a big slow cooker, make a bigger batch and have leftovers to freeze for another time!

3. French Onion Soup

Serves: 6

Preparation time: 20 minutes + 3 hours cooking time

Ingredients:

- ☐ 8 cups beef broth
- ☐ 4 onions
- ☐ 4 garlic cloves
- ☐ 4 tablespoons butter
- ☐ 1 bay leaf

Direction:

1) Peel the onion and chop it into rings. Add it into a pan with the butter to begin softening. Have them cooking for 10-15 minutes to caramelise nicely.
2) Peel and mince the garlic and add it into the slow cooker, along with the beef broth and bay leaf.
3) Add the onions into the slow cooker too and season with salt and pepper. Cook on High for 3 hours.
4) Remove the bay leaf and serve.

Serving Suggestion: A slice of crusty French bread with cheese is exactly what you need to be dipping into this soup. 15

minutes before you're about to serve your soup, place slices of crusty French bread onto a baking tray and top each with slices of Swiss cheese. Broil until the cheese is melted.

Tip: If you have shallots, use some of them too for a little bit of extra flavour.

4. Pea Soup

Serves: 6
Preparation time: 10 minutes + 6 hours cooking time

Ingredients:

- [ ] 16 oz split peas
- [ ] 2 stalks celery
- [ ] 1 leek
- [ ] 1/2 cup frozen garden peas
- [ ] 2/3 cup fresh parsley

Direction:

1) Tie the stems of the parsley together and place it into the slow cooker.
2) Clean and chop up the leek and celery and add them into the pot tpp, along with the split peas and garden peas.
3) Season well with salt and pepper, and add 7 cups of water.
4) Cook for 6 hours on Low.

Serving Suggestion: Topping with a little yoghurt or sour cream and ham hock is a fantastic way to enjoy this dish!

Tip: If you like, blend half of the soup and keep the other half chunky, or puree the whole thing, depending on your preference.

5. Chicken Noodle Soup

Serves: 6

Preparation time: 30 minutes + 5 hours cooking time

Ingredients:

3 carrots
3 cups egg noodles
2 bay leaves
1 whole chicken
1 onion

Direction:

Peel and dice the carrots and onion.
Place the whole chicken on top of the vegetables and add in the bay leaves and 8 cups of water.
Season the soup well with salt and pepper.
Cook on High for 4-1/2 hours, and then remove the chicken.
Place the noodles into the broth, and re-cover the cooker.
Remove the skin and shred the chicken.
Then, replace the chicken and cook for a further 5-10 minutes, until the noodles are cooked through.

Serving Suggestion: This has to be on the coldest of cold days, and is best enjoyed in front of a fire, under a blanket and in your most comfortable slippers!

Tip: Freeze any leftovers for those emergency sick days – we all know there's no cure like chicken noodle soup!

6. Turkey & Black Bean Soup

Serves: 6

Preparation time: 30 minutes + 6 hours cooking time

Ingredients:

- [ ] 24 oz turkey drumstick
- [ ] 16 oz dried black beans
- [ ] 4 garlic cloves
- [ ] 3 carrots
- [ ] 2 red onions

Direction:

1) Set aside half of one of the onions and peel and dice the rest of it. Begin softening the onion in a pan.
2) Mince in the garlic too.
3) Peel and chop the carrot and add it to the pan.
4) After 5 minutes or so, add in 2 tablespoons of water, and season well with salt and pepper. Use a spoon to scrape up any burnt bits.
5) Rinse the bean, and pick out any bad ones.
6) Pour all of the contents of the pan into the slow cooker and add in the beans and the turkey.
7) Add in 8 cups of water, and season again with salt and pepper. Leave the soup cooking on Low for 6 hours.
8) Remove the turkey drumstick from the soup and set it aside to shred.
9) Take out 2 cups of the beans and blend until smooth.
10) Return the blended beans and shredded turkey to the slow cooker.
11) Dice up the remaining half of the onion and stir it through the soup before serving.

Serving Suggestion: Serve with a dollop of sour cream and fresh cilantro and lime wedges.

Tip: If you're into your spice, add in red chilli flakes to the soup.

7. Cauliflower Soup

Serves: 6

Preparation time: 30 minutes + 6 hours cooking time

Ingredients:

- 4 cups chicken or vegetable broth
- 1 head cauliflower
- 1 onion
- 1 tablespoon butter
- 1 tablespoon plain flour

Direction:

1) Begin melting the butter in a pan.
2) Then, stir in the flour until you have a thick, smooth roux.
3) Peel and dice the onion and add it to the roux to begin softening.
4) Chop the cauliflower into small pieces and add it into the slow cooker.
5) Pour in the roux and chicken broth. Season well with salt and pepper.
6) Cook on Low for 6 hours.
7) Then, blend it up until smooth.
8)

Serving Suggestion: Serve topped with shredded cheese,

green onions and crumbled bacon.

Tip: If you're not too concerned about the calories and are just looking for some awesome creamy soup, add in 1 cup of heavy cream, and stir shredded cheese into the soup too.

8. Kale & Chorizo Soup

Serves: 6

Preparation time: 10 minutes + 6 hours cooking time

Ingredients:

- 16 oz chorizo
- 15 oz canned tomatoes
- 4 garlic cloves
- 4 cups vegetable broth
- 1 bunch kale

Direction:

1) Into the slow cooker, add the canned tomatoes and vegetable broth.
2) De-stem the kale and mince the garlic.
3) Add everything into the slow cooker and season well with salt and pepper.
4) Cook on Low for 6 hours.
5) Take the chorizo out and 'mash' it. Place it back into the slow cooker and stir well before serving.

Serving Suggestion: This is what we like to call 'hearty' soup, so fresh, crusty bread is really the only way forward!

Tip: Bulk this out more by adding in sweet potatoes.

9. Chicken Stock

Makes: 3 quarts

Preparation time: 5 minutes + 4 hours cooking time

Ingredients:

- ☐ 2 carrots
- ☐ 2 celery sticks
- ☐ 1 whole chicken
- ☐ 1 onion
- ☐ 1 bunch fresh thyme

Direction:

1) Place the whole chicken into the slow cooker.
2) Peel and chop the carrots, celery and onion.
3) Place all of the vegetables into the slow cooker, along with the thyme.
4) Pour in 128 fl oz of water, and season well with salt and pepper.
5) Cook for 8 hours on Low.
6) Keep the chicken for use in other recipes, and strain the stock into your storing container.

Serving Suggestion: Well, now you have delicious chicken stock for a tonne of recipes! You can use this as a base for some of the soup recipes in this book!

Tip: Add in other fresh herbs too, if you like. Rosemary, oregano and sage all work deliciously.

10. Tomato & Basil Tortellini Soup

Serves: 8

Preparation time: 15 minutes + 6 hours cooking time

Ingredients:

- 84 oz canned whole tomatoes
- 16 oz tortellini
- 5 garlic cloves
- 3/4 cup heavy cream
- 1/3 cup fresh basil + extra to garnish

Direction:

1) Peel and mince the garlic and begin softening it in a pan.
2) Then, add them into the slow cooker along with the canned tomatoes and 32 fl oz of water. Season well with salt and pepper.
3) Tear up the basil and stir it in. Cook on High for 6 hours.
4) Blend the soup up until smooth.
5) Then, stir in the tortellini and cook for a further 15 minutes.
6) Stir in the cream and garnish with extra basil to serve.

Serving Suggestion: Is it just me, or is tomato soup just so much more homely and amazing when in a large mug? Just set yourself up in the perfect position under a blanket, in your cosiest slippers and with a mug of this soup.

Tip: For extra flavour, use vegetable broth in place of the water when making soups.

11. Sausage & Pearl Barley Soup

Serves: 4

Preparation time: 15 minutes + 8 hours cooking time

Ingredients:

- 48 fl oz chicken broth
- 16 oz Italian sausage
- 1 onion
- 1 teaspoon dried Italian herbs
- 1/4 cup uncooked pearl barley

Direction:

1) Peel and dice the onion and add it into a pan to begin to soften. Slice up the sausage and add it into the pan too.
2) Stir the Italian herbs into the pan, and then pour everything into the slow cooker.
3) Then, pour in the chicken broth and stir in the pearl barley.
4) Cook on Low for 8 hours.

Serving Suggestion: Go all domesticated and bake your own herby Italian bread to dunk into this delicious soup.

Tip: As ever with soup, you can bulk it up and make it go further by adding in extra veggies.

12. Clam Chowder

Serves: 4-6

Preparation time: 15 minutes + 8 hours cooking time

Ingredients:

- 26 oz canned clams & juice
- 4 large potatoes
- 4 oz bacon
- 2 cups milk
- 1 onion

Direction:

1) Peel and dice the onion and begin browning it in a pan, along with the bacon.
2) Drain the clams, keeping the juice, and add the clams into the slow cooker.
3) Crumble up the bacon and add the bacon and onions to the cooker too.
4) Peel and chop up the potatoes and add them in.
5) Pour in the clam liquid, season with salt and pepper, and cook on High for 3-1/2 hours.
6) Then, add in the milk and cook for an additional 5 minutes, adjusting the seasoning, before serving.

Serving Suggestion: My first clam chowder experience was actually a very special one, in San Francisco, where they famously serve clam chowder in sourdough bread bowls! So, if you have the time and knowhow, try making some bread bowls yourself and it'll be adorable!

Tip: If you prefer a blended up soup, do so, just keep the bacon aside and just crumble it on top with some cheese.

13. Borsch<u>t</u>

Serves: 4-6

Preparation time: 10 minutes + 8-1/2 hours cooking time

Ingredients:

- ☐ 8 cups beef broth
- ☐ 4 large beetroots
- ☐ 3 tablespoons red wine vinegar
- ☐ 2 large potatoes
- ☐ 2 cups cabbage

Direction:

1) Peel and chop up the beetroots and potatoes and add them into the slow cooker.
2) Then, pour in the beef broth and red wine vinegar. Season with salt and pepper to taste, and cook on Low for 8 hours.
3) Then, shred up the cabbage and add it in to cook on High for a final 30 minutes before serving.

Serving Suggestion: Just a little dollop of sour cream or crème fraiche for some creaminess is all you need with this delicious borscht.

Tip: An easy way to peel beetroots is by pre-boiling them and then running them under cold water whilst rubbing off the skin.

14. Cream of Mushroom Soup

Serves: 6

Preparation time: 20 minutes + 4 ½ hours cooking time

Ingredients:

- 6 cups mushrooms
- 3 garlic cloves
- 1 cup dry white wine
- 1 cup heavy cream
- 1/4 cup corn starch

Direction:

1) Peel and mince the garlic and add it to a pan to begin to soften.
2) Peel and chop up the mushrooms, and add them to the pan with the garlic.
3) Add the white wine into the pan and allow it to cook down for 2 minutes, before pouring the whole thing into the slow cooker.
4) Pour in 4 cups of water, well seasoned with salt and pepper, and cook on Low for 4 hours.
5) Whisk together the cream and cornstarch until thick, and stir it into the soup.

6) Season again, to taste, and cook on High for another 30 minutes.
7) Remove half of the soup and blend it until smooth. Stir it back in with the rest of the soup and enjoy!

Serving Suggestion: This is such a winter warming soup! Bake your own fresh sundried tomato bread and get dunking!

Tip: If you're looking for a way to use up those weird cans you have in the pantry, then canned mushrooms work just as well in this dish!

15. Bone Broth

Serves: 8

Preparation time: 15 minutes + 8 hours cooking time

Ingredients:

- ☐ 32 oz bones
- ☐ 6 oz tomato paste
- ☐ 3 garlic cloves
- ☐ 3 bay leaves
- ☐ 2 onions

Direction:

1) Preheat the oven to 400F.
2) Spread the bones out on a baking tray and spread the tomato paste on over the top of them. Sprinkle on salt and pepper.
3) Bake for 30-40 minutes, until the bones are browning and giving

off a roasting smell.
4) Transfer everything into your slow cooker, and add water it until it covers the bones up to 1 inch over the top.
5) Peel and dice the onion and garlic, and add them into the slow cooker, along with the bay leaves.
6) Cook on Low for 24 hours, and strain the broth into sterilised jars to refrigerate.

Serving Suggestion: This broth makes a delicious base for many a soup or stew!

Tip: Don't go out and buy bones especially! Simply freeze bones from whatever you're cooking until you have enough to make your broth.

16. Broccoli & Stilton Soup

Serves: 4

Preparation time: 15 minutes + 8 hours cooking time

Ingredients:

- [ ] 32 fl oz chicken stock
- [ ] 5-1/2 oz stilton
- [ ] 1 whole head of broccoli
- [ ] 1 onion
- [ ] 1 large potato

Direction:

1) Chop the broccoli into florets, and peel and dice the potato and onion.
2) Add the vegetables into the slow cooker, and crumble in the stilton.
3) Pour the chicken stock into the slow cooker, and season with salt and pepper to taste.
4) Cook on Low for 8 hours.
5) Leave the soup to cool a little, and then blend until smooth.

Serving Suggestion: Well, more cheese crumbled on top can hardly be a bad thing, can it?

Tip: Maybe if you're making this as a family meal, and your kids' palettes aren't quite ready for strong stilton yet, then cheddar is a milder but just as yummy option instead.

17. Carrot & Coriander Soup

Serves: 4

Preparation time: 15 minutes + 8 hours cooking time

Ingredients:

- ☐ 21 oz carrots
- ☐ 1 onion
- ☐ 1 stick of celery
- ☐ 1 garlic cloves
- ☐ 1 teaspoon ground coriander seeds + fresh coriander to garnish

Direction:

1) Peel and chop the carrots and add them into the slow cooker.
2) Peel and dice the onion and celery and add them into the cooker too.
3) Mince in the garlic, and sprinkle in the ground coriander, along with a good pinch of salt and pepper.
4) Pour in 16 fl oz of water and cook on Low for 8 hours.
5) Blend the soup until smooth and sue the fresh coriander to garnish as you serve.

Serving Suggestion: If you're a crazy person and want to eat soup when it's hot, then this one could be for you! Actually, freshly squeezed lemonade is a lovely cool, long drink to have on the side.

Tip: Weigh the carrots after you've peeled them. Otherwise, you may end up with not enough!

18. Leek & Potato Soup

Serves: 6

Preparation time: 15 minutes + 6 hours cooking time

Ingredients:

- [ ] 5 cups vegetable broth
- [ ] 4 large potatoes
- [ ] 3 carrots
- [ ] 3 leeks
- [ ] 3 garlic cloves

Direction:

1) Peel and dice the potatoes, carrots and leeks and peel and mince the garlic. Add them all into the slow cooker.
2) Pour in the vegetable broth and season with salt and pepper.
3) Cook on Low for 6 hours, and then blend the soup up before serving.

Serving Suggestion: This is actually a very low calorie option, so why ruin it with a tonne of cream? If you like that creamy swirl on top of your soup, try using low fat crème fraiche or Greek yoghurt instead.

Tip: For some extra flavour in your soup, brown your leeks in a pan first before adding them into the slow cooker. You can then keep some of the rings aside to use as a garnish.

19. Fish Stock

Makes: 50 fl oz

Preparation time: 10 minutes + 8 hours cooking time

Ingredients:

- [ ] 6 black peppercorns
- [ ] 2 celery stalks
- [ ] 1 whole fish carcass
- [ ] 1 onion
- [ ] 1 small bunch fresh parsley

Direction:

1) Peel and dice the onion and celery, and begin softening them in a pan.
2) Add the vegetables into the slow cooker, and add in the parsley and peppercorns.
3) Lay the fish carcass on top of everything, and pour in 65 fl oz of water.
4) Season well with salt and pepper and leave cooking on Low for 8 hours.
5) Strain the broth into a sterilised jar and keep refrigerated until needed.

Serving Suggestion: This makes a great base for many a Thai dish. Try making a Thai green curry based on this fish stock, Thai green curry paste and coconut milk – delicious!

Tip: If you have a specific dish in mind for making with this broth, then you can already add spices and herbs that you'll need.

20. Rosemary Lentil Soup

Makes: 6

Preparation time: 15 minutes + 6 hours cooking time

Ingredients:

- ☐ 6 carrots
- ☐ 4 garlic cloves
- ☐ 3 cups red lentils
- ☐ 1 yellow bell pepper
- ☐ 1 bunch fresh rosemary + 1 teaspoon dried rosemary

Direction:

1) De-seed and chop the yellow bell pepper, peel and chop the carrots and peel and mince the garlic cloves. Add them into the slow cooker.
2) Add the lentils into the slow cooker too, and pour in 2-3/4 cups of water.
3) Season well with salt and pepper and leave the soup cooking on Low for 5 hours.
4) Then, add in the fresh and dried rosemary and leave it cooking for another hour.
5) Take out the bunch of rosemary, and blend the soup before serving.

Serving Suggestion: For an added kick, sprinkle some chilli powder on top of the soup.

Tip: If you like to have some whole lentils, then don't blend the soup, but just be aware to chop the vegetables up small enough to start with.

The Final Words

Thanks again for reading this easy slow cooker cookbook. Hope you have found your favorite recipes which is time-saving and money-saving. Best wishes to you! Dear readers!

Printed in Great Britain
by Amazon